Simple
Style

Simple Style

Easy Weekend Quilts

Sara Diepersloot

Martingale®
& COMPANY

Simple Style: Easy Weekend Quilts
© 2009 by Sara Diepersloot

That Patchwork Place® is an imprint of
Martingale & Company®.

Martingale & Company
20205 144th Ave. NE
Woodinville, WA 98072-8478 USA
www.martingale-pub.com

Printed in China
14 13 12 11 10 09   8 7 6 5 4 3 2 1

**Library of Congress Cataloging-in-Publication Data
is available upon request.**

ISBN: 978-1-56477-949-6

Mission Statement

Dedicated to providing quality products and service to inspire creativity.

Credits

President & CEO: Tom Wierzbicki

Editor in Chief: Mary V. Green

Managing Editor: Tina Cook

Developmental Editor: Karen Costello Soltys

Technical Editor: Ellen Pahl

Copy Editor: Melissa Bryan

Design Director: Stan Green

Production Manager: Regina Girard

Illustrators: Adrienne Smitke & Laurel Strand

Cover & Text Designer: Stan Green

Photographer: Brent Kane

Dedication

To my grandparents, Ed and Betty Morgan. You have always been such an important part of my life, and so many of my favorite memories include the two of you. Weekends spent at your house as a young girl were the best—picking berries, feeding horses, working on projects in the car barn, tea parties in the tree house, Gram reading us a favorite bedtime story, and jumping into bed with you in the morning to hear Grandy's silly stories! And don't forget Gram's homemade chocolate milkshakes—yummm, they were the best.

You have always believed in me and encouraged me. You enabled me to go to design school and start my own business. You were both *so* excited for me when you heard about this book.

Grandy, I think just a touch of your creativity and ingenuity got passed down to me. You could always figure out how to piece something together and make it work. I do it on a much smaller scale with my quilts. (He designed and built most of the original rides at Disneyland!) Gram, you have always been one of my best friends. Thank you for always being there to talk to when I need it; I love spending time with you.

You both have always lavished your grandkids and great-grandkids with so much love. We are truly blessed to have you. I love you both so much!

Acknowledgments

My thanks go to:

My amazing husband, Rodney. Thanks for all the extra help with the kids, dishes, etc., so that I could finish this book on time. I couldn't have done it without you! You have been my biggest fan. Thanks for always believing in me!

My beautiful kids, Laura, Kimmie, Ryan, and David. You are all so creative and inspire me every day. Thanks for filling our house with laughter and fun!

My wonderful quilting angels, Deborah Rasmussen and Renae Gleason. These two ladies worked on five of my quilts and did an amazing job. Deborah, your long-arm quilting is beautiful! Renae, I've never seen binding so perfect! Thank you, thank you, both so much. Without you I never would have made my deadline!

Judy, John, Nina, and the ladies at Judy's Sewing Center. Thanks for your wonderful classes, where I first learned to quilt, and for your great quilt shop that always inspires me! But most of all, thank you for your friendship and kindness, and the special hugs you always have for my kids!

Karen Soltys, thank you so much for guiding me through the process of writing a book, and for your helpfulness and kind words of encouragement.

Ellen Pahl, my amazing technical editor. Thank you for finding my silly mistakes and making all of my instructions perfect! You have taught me a lot along the way. You are SO good at what you do!

Melissa Bryan, thank you for taking some of my jumbled-up wording and making sense out of it!

Cathy Reitan and all of the staff at Martingale & Company for making this experience of writing a book so wonderful. You have been amazing to work with!

Contents

Introduction ~ 11

Basic Quiltmaking
    Techniques ~ 12

THE QUILTS ~ 16

Grown-Up Girls ~ 19

Picnic Time ~ 21

Asian Squares ~ 25

Black & White ~ 27

Bunnies in My Garden ~ 31

Surf's Up, Baby! ~ 33

Summertime ~ 37

Pineapple Paradise ~ 39

Cherry Blossoms ~ 43

Batik Squares ~ 47

Batik Addiction ~ 49

Quick Bricks ~ 53

Christmas Stars ~ 55

Hidden Stars ~ 59

Squares Around ~ 63

Simple Scrap
    Table Runner ~ 65

Tilted Squares
    Table Runner ~ 67

Cherries
    Table Runner ~ 69

Sweet Treats ~ 71

I Love Recess! ~ 75

About the Author ~ 79

Introduction

I love fabric! Give me a day of shopping in my favorite quilt shops, or discovering new ones, and I'm in heaven! I'm especially drawn to fun novelty prints and amazing large-scale prints that are becoming more and more popular today.

Most of the quilts I designed for this book were inspired by these fabrics. I tend to buy my "focus fabric" first, and then search out just the right fabrics to go with it. I love to pull colors and textures together until my palette is just right.

I also love to design quilts that are simple enough to show off these fabrics, and that I can actually finish in a reasonable amount of time. Many quilters today don't have a lot of extra time in their busy schedules, and a quilt with 500 tiny triangles just isn't going to happen! I have four kids at home, so I definitely need projects that are quick and easy. And I definitely need a creative outlet to help keep my sanity! I love those couple of quiet hours at night after all the children are in bed when I can take a deep breath and enjoy creating something beautiful.

I hope you are inspired by the quilts in this book to make something beautiful too!

Fabulous fabrics provided the inspiration for most of the quilts in this book.

Basic Quiltmaking Techniques

The quilts in this book are all very easy and were made using standard quiltmaking techniques: machine piecing, rotary cutting, and machine quilting. If you need additional guidance in any of those areas, please consider taking a class at your favorite quilt shop, or consult some of the many excellent books that cover quiltmaking in greater detail.

Seam Allowances

One of the most important aspects of quiltmaking is having an accurate ¼" seam allowance. If your seam allowances aren't accurate, your quilt will not fit together well and you will be frustrated! Many sewing machines today have a ¼" quilting foot that allows you to use the edge of the foot as a guide.

An easy test to see if your ¼" seam allowance is accurate is to take three 2"-wide scraps and sew them together. Press the seam allowances to one side, and measure the center piece. It should measure 1½" wide. If it does not, adjust your seam allowance accordingly.

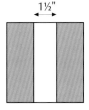

Making Straight-Set Quilts

Many of the quilts in this book feature straight settings—blocks arranged in horizontal rows that are then sewn together. Follow the steps below to sew the blocks together.

1. Arrange the blocks of your quilt as shown in the illustrations for the project you are making.

2. Sew the blocks together into horizontal rows. Press the seam allowances toward the setting blocks, if applicable. If the blocks are all pieced, press seam allowances in the opposite direction from row to row.

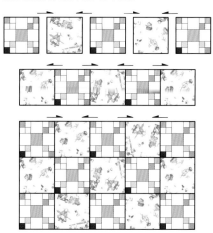

3. Sew the rows together. Press all the seam allowances in one direction.

Making Diagonally Set Quilts

These quilts require side and corner setting triangles. The cutting dimensions for all the setting triangles in this book are slightly oversized. This allows you to square up your quilt top before adding the borders.

1. Arrange the blocks and setting triangles of your quilt as shown in the illustrations for the project you are making.

2. Sew the blocks together in diagonal rows. Press the seam allowances in the opposite direction from row to row (or toward setting blocks).

MAKING A DESIGN WALL

I love using a design wall. If you have some wall space, you can easily make one of your own. I used two 32" x 40" sheets of foamboard (available at art-supply stores) and covered them with inexpensive white flannel. I stretched the flannel over the foamboard and used hot glue to adhere the edges down on the back. I placed the boards right next to each other and used a nail gun to attach them to the wall.

The foamboard is great because you can stick pins in it, and the flannel is perfect for "holding" the fabrics. Most of the time, I can simply put my fabric pieces right on the design wall, and the flannel will hold it without needing any pins. I use my design wall to "audition" which fabrics I will use in a quilt. I find it especially helpful when I am making a scrappy quilt, because I can easily arrange and rearrange the fabrics to make sure that the colors are balanced throughout the quilt.

3. Sew the rows together. Press all the seam allowances in one direction. Add the corner setting triangles last and press toward the triangles.

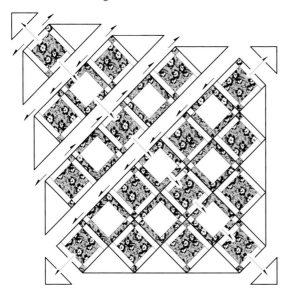

4. Square up each side of the quilt top, lining up the ¼" mark on your ruler with the block points and trimming the quilt edges. This gives you a perfect ¼" seam allowance. Square up the corners to 90° angles; a large square ruler is very helpful for this.

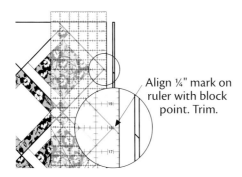

Align ¼" mark on ruler with block point. Trim.

Adding Borders

When you're measuring your quilt to determine the length of the borders, measure through the center of the quilt. Often the edges of your quilt have stretched slightly and can differ in size from one side to the other. By measuring through the center of the quilt, you will get accurate borders that lie flat. The project instructions will tell you how many 42"-long strips to cut. Piece the strips together to create one long strip.

1. Measure the length of the quilt top through the center from top to bottom. Cut two border pieces to this length for the sides of your quilt. Mark the center of the quilt and the center of each border strip. Match the centers and ends, and sew the border strips to the sides of the quilt, easing to fit if necessary. Press the seam allowances toward the borders.

2. Measure the width of the quilt top through the center from side to side, including the side borders you just added. Cut two border pieces to this length. Mark the center of the quilt and the center of the border strips. Sew the border strips to the top and bottom edges of the quilt, easing to fit if necessary. Press seam allowances toward the borders.

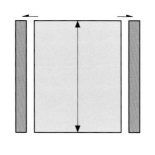
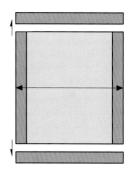

Layering and Basting

I have a long-arm quilting machine, so I don't usually need to layer and baste my quilts. Many quilters today choose to send their quilt tops to a professional long-arm quilter. If you do this, ask your quilter for any specific instructions on how to prepare the quilt top. Typically, you will need to give them a backing piece that is about 4" larger than the quilt top on all sides. You will not need to layer or baste your quilt; the long-arm machine does this for you.

If you choose to do the machine quilting yourself, find a table or even a wood floor that is big enough to lay out your entire quilt. Smooth out the quilt backing, right side down, and tape it down with masking tape to hold it in place. Next, smooth the batting out over the quilt backing. Finally, center the pressed quilt top over the backing and batting and smooth it out, making sure there are no wrinkles in any of the layers.

Using quilting safety pins, pin the quilt every 4" to 6", trying to avoid placing pins right where you are going to quilt.

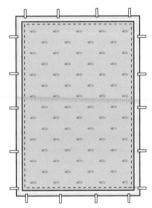

Binding

I use 2¼"-wide strips for my bindings. All the instructions in this book will specify the number of binding strips you will need to cut, typically determined by the measurement around the quilt plus about 10" for corners and overlap.

1. Sew the binding strips together along the diagonal to create one long strip. Trim seam allowances and press them open. Fold the binding strip in half lengthwise with wrong sides together and press.

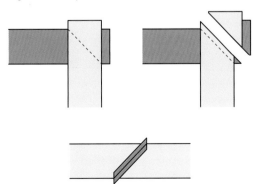

2. Place the binding about two thirds of the way down one side of the front of the quilt, with the raw edges even. Leaving a 5" tail and using a ¼" seam allowance, sew the binding to the quilt. Sew until you are ¼" from the corner of the quilt. Backstitch and remove the quilt from the machine.

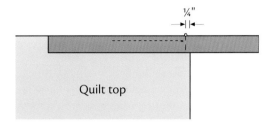

Quilt top

3. Fold the binding strip up at a 45° angle from the quilt. Then fold it back down so that it is even with the next side as shown. Start sewing at the top edge of the quilt. Continue sewing around the quilt, repeating the mitering at each corner.

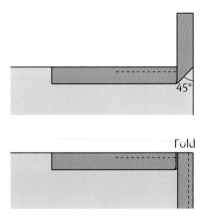

45°

Fold

4. When you are about 10" from where you started, remove the quilt from the machine. Fold back the beginning and ending tails of the binding so that they meet in the center. Finger-press the folded edges.

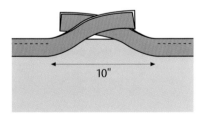

10"

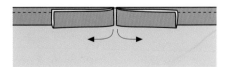

5. Unfold both ends of the binding and match the center points of the two folds, forming an X as shown. Pin and sew the two ends together on the diagonal of the fold lines. Trim ¼" from the sewing line. Press the seam allowances open and refold the binding. Continue sewing the binding to the quilt.

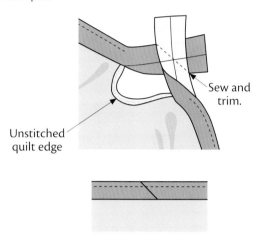

Unstitched quilt edge

Sew and trim.

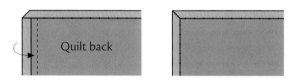

6. Fold the binding to the back of the quilt over the raw edges. The corners will fold into beautiful miters. The binding should just cover the stitching line. Hand stitch the binding in place.

Quilt back

Hanging Sleeve

If you'd like to hang your quilt, I suggest adding a hanging sleeve just before adding the binding.

1. Cut a piece of fabric that's 8" wide and 1" shorter than the width of your quilt, piecing it for the width if necessary. You can use the same fabric as the backing if there is enough left over, or use a coordinating fabric from your stash.

2. Fold each 8" end under ½" two times and machine sew along the edge to create a hem.

Fold ends under ½" twice.

BINDING ODD ANGLES

Attaching the binding to table runners that have odd angles is very similar to dealing with 90° corners. Simply stop stitching when you reach the point where seams will intersect, and backstitch. Fold the binding up to create a 45° angle as you normally would. Keeping the 45° fold in place, fold the binding strip down so that the raw edges align with the next side to be sewn. Begin sewing at the point where you stopped sewing; sew forward a few stitches, then backstitch to secure the miter. Sew forward and continue sewing the binding on.

3. Fold the fabric in half lengthwise with wrong sides together. Baste or pin the raw edges to the top of the quilt along the backing. The top edge of the sleeve will be stitched when the binding is sewn to the quilt.

Baste sleeve to top edge of quilt.

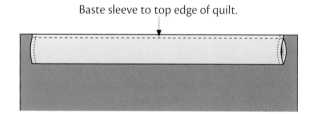

4. Blindstitch the side and bottom edges in place after the binding is complete. Push the bottom edge of the sleeve up about ¼" to ½" as you sew; this will provide some extra space for the hanging rod and minimize strain on the quilt.

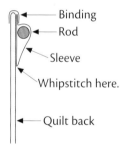

Binding
Rod
Sleeve
Whipstitch here.
Quilt back

Labels

Don't forget to label your quilts when you're done with them. You can personalize a label with your name and date, the name of the recipient, and even the name of the quilt if you have one. What a great way for generations to come to know when and where your quilt was made.

You can use a small piece of white cotton fabric for the label and write the information in permanent ink. Add some artwork or even embroidery. You can even make a small pieced label if you'd like. Then, turn under the edges and hand sew to the back of your quilt. The possibilities are endless!

The Quilts

Page 19

Page 21

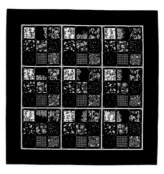

Page 25

Page 27

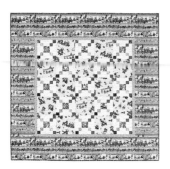

Page 31

Page 33

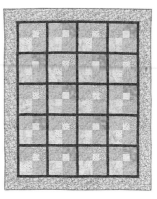

Page 37

Page 39

Page 43

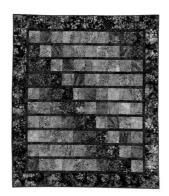

Page 47

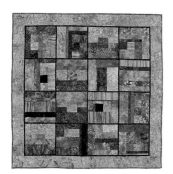

Page 49

Page 53

Page 55

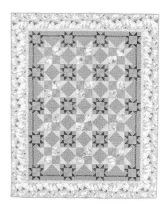

Page 59

Page 63

Page 65

Page 71

Page 75

Page 67

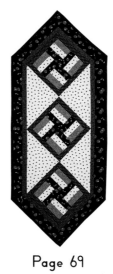

Page 69

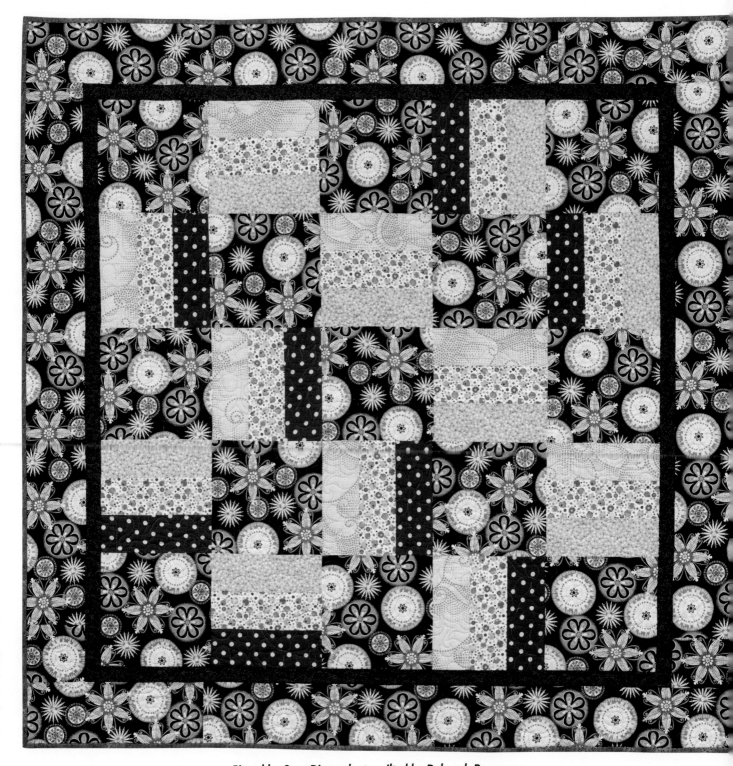

Pieced by Sara Diepersloot, quilted by Deborah Rasmussen

Grown-Up Girls

I've made this quick quilt several times as gifts for my daughters, nieces, and friends. It's a great size to cuddle up in.

Finished Quilt: 58" x 58"
Finished Block: 9" x 9"

Materials

Yardage is based on 42"-wide fabric.

2¼ yards of brown floral for setting blocks and outer border

⅜ yard of pink-and-green print for Rail Fence blocks

⅓ yard of brown fabric for inner border

¼ yard of green print for Rail Fence blocks

¼ yard of pink print for Rail Fence blocks

¼ yard of brown-and-pink polka-dot fabric for Rail Fence blocks

⅝ yard of fabric for binding

3⅝ yards of fabric for backing

64" x 64" piece of batting

Cutting

From the pink-and-green print, cut:
3 strips, 3½" x 42"

From the green print, cut:
2 strips, 3½" x 42"

From the pink print, cut:
2 strips, 3½" x 42"

From the brown-and-pink polka-dot fabric, cut:
2 strips, 3½" x 42"

From the brown floral, cut:
4 strips, 9½" x 42"; crosscut into 13 squares, 9½" x 9½"
6 strips, 5½" x 42"

From the brown fabric, cut:
5 strips, 1¾" x 42"

From the binding fabric, cut:
7 strips, 2¼" x 42"

Making the Blocks

1. Using the 3½"-wide strips, join one strip each of the pink print, the pink-and-green print, and the polka-dot fabric to make strip set A. Crosscut the strip set into four 9½"-wide blocks.

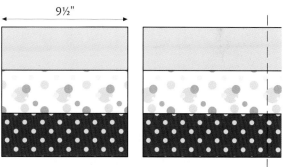

Strip set A.
Make 1. Cut 4 blocks.

2. Join one strip each of the pink print, the pink-and-green print, and the green print to make strip set B. Crosscut the strip set into four 9½"-wide blocks.

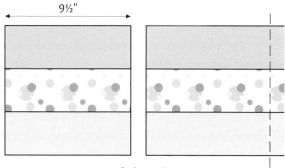

Strip set B.
Make 1. Cut 4 blocks.

3. Join one strip each of the polka-dot fabric, the pink-and-green print, and the green print to make strip set C. Crosscut the strip set into four 9½"-wide blocks.

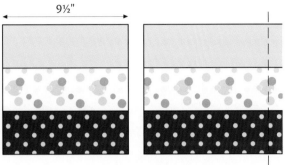

9½"

Strip set C.
Make 1. Cut 4 blocks.

Quilt-Top Assembly

1. Sew the brown floral squares and the Rail Fence blocks together into rows, alternating the orientation of the Rail Fence blocks as shown in the quilt diagram. Join the rows.

2. Referring to "Adding Borders" on page 13, attach the inner and outer borders.

3. Layer the quilt top with batting and backing, and quilt as desired.

4. Referring to "Binding" on page 14, bind the edges of the quilt.

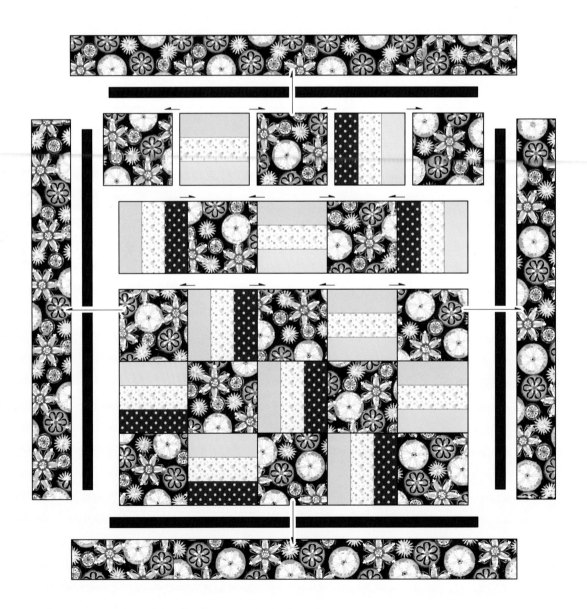

Picnic Time

This fabric collection is wonderful. Do you see the tiny ants in the inner border, and the watermelon rind fabric for the binding? Perfect for a picnic at the park!

Finished Quilt: 58" x 58"
Finished Block: 6" x 6"

Materials

Yardage is based on 42"-wide fabric.

1¾ yards of watermelon print for blocks and outer border

⅞ yard of black dot fabric for blocks

⅞ yard of green dot fabric for blocks

¾ yard of red seed print for blocks

⅓ yard of red checked fabric for inner border

¼ yard of green print for middle border

⅝ yard of fabric for binding

3⅝ yards of fabric for backing

64" x 64" piece of batting

Cutting

From the black dot fabric, cut:
3 strips, 3½" x 42"

2 strips, 7½" x 42"; crosscut into 6 squares, 7½" x 7½". Cut the squares once diagonally to make 12 triangles.

From the green dot fabric, cut:
3 strips, 3½" x 42"

2 strips, 7½" x 42"; crosscut into 6 squares, 7½" x 7½". Cut the squares once diagonally to make 12 triangles.

From the red seed print, cut:
3 strips, 7½" x 42"; crosscut into 12 squares, 7½" x 7½". Cut the squares once diagonally to make 24 triangles.

From the watermelon print, cut:
2 strips, 6½" x 42"; crosscut into 9 squares, 6½" x 6½"

6 strips, 6½" x 42"

From the red checked fabric, cut:
5 strips, 1½" x 42"

From the green print, cut:
5 strips, 1¼" x 42"

From the binding fabric, cut:
7 strips, 2¼" x 42"

Making the Four Patch Blocks

1. Sew each 3½"-wide black dot strip to a 3½"-wide green dot strip to make three strip sets. Crosscut the strip sets into 32 segments, 3½" wide.

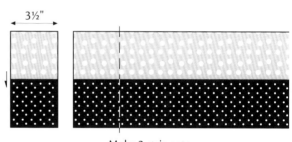

Make 3 strip sets.
Cut 32 segments.

2. Sew two 3½" segments together to make a Four Patch block. Make 16 Four Patch blocks.

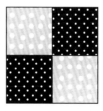

Make 16.

Pieced and quilted by Sara Diepersloot

Making the Hourglass Blocks

1. Sew a green dot triangle to a red seed print triangle. Press the seam allowances toward the red. Make 12. Sew a black dot triangle to a red seed print triangle. Press the seam allowances toward the red. Make 12.

Make 12.   Make 12.

2. Cut the units from step 1 once diagonally.

3. Sew a green-and-red unit to a black-and-red unit, making sure the reds are opposite each other. Make 24 Hourglass blocks. These units will be oversized. Square them up to 6½" square.

Make 24.

Quilt-Top Assembly

1. Join the Four Patch blocks, Hourglass blocks, and watermelon squares into rows as shown. Sew the rows together.

2. Referring to "Adding Borders" on page 13, attach the inner, middle, and outer borders.

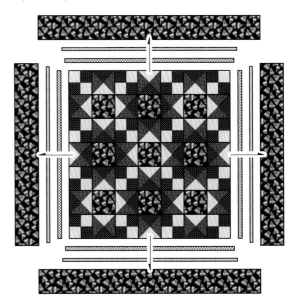

3. Layer the quilt top with batting and backing, and quilt as desired.

4. Referring to "Binding" on page 14, bind the edges of the quilt.

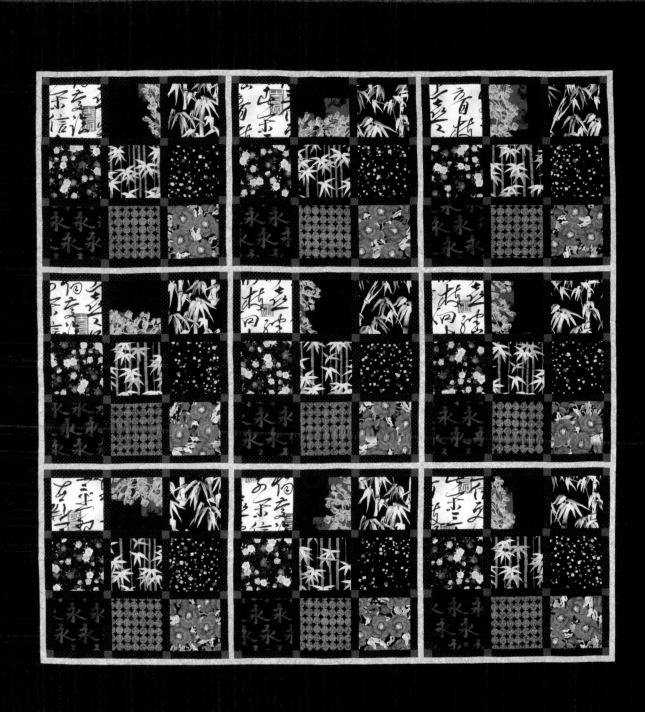

Pieced and quilted by Sara Diepersloot

Asian Squares

I've always loved red-and-black quilts. This one really pops with the touch of green for the sashing. These beautiful fabrics just begged to come home from the fabric store with me!

Finished Quilt: 69½" x 69½"
Finished Block: 18" x 18"

Materials

Yardage is based on 42"-wide fabric.

⅜ yard *each* of 9 different Asian prints for blocks

1⅝ yards of black print for border

1⅜ yards of black dot fabric for blocks

½ yard of bright green print for sashing

⅓ yard of red print for blocks

⅝ yard of fabric for binding

4½ yards of fabric for backing

76" x 76" piece of batting

Cutting

From the red print, cut:
6 strips, 1¼" x 42"; crosscut 2 strips into 36 squares, 1¼" x 1¼"

From the black dot fabric, cut:
8 strips, 5½" x 42"; crosscut 4 strips into 108 rectangles, 1¼" x 5½"

From *each* of the 9 Asian prints, cut:
2 strips, 5½" x 42"; crosscut into 9 squares, 5½" x 5½"

From the bright green print, cut:
12 strips, 1" x 42"; crosscut 3 strips into 6 sashing strips, 1" x 18½"

From the black print, cut:
7 strips, 7" x 42"

From the binding fabric, cut:
7 strips, 2¼" x 42"

Making the Blocks

Before you begin, decide on the placement of your Asian fabrics within the block. In my quilt, I kept the fabrics in the same position in each block.

1. Sew one 1¼" red strip to one 5½" black dot strip. Press the seam allowances toward the red. Make four strip sets. Crosscut into 108 segments, 1¼" wide.

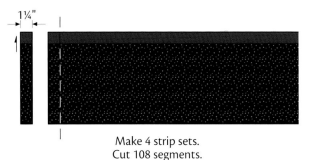

Make 4 strip sets.
Cut 108 segments.

2. Join three segments from step 1 with one red square to make a row. Press the seam allowances toward the red square. Make 36 rows.

Make 36.

3. Join four black dot rectangles and three Asian print squares to make a row. Make three rows per block, paying close attention to the placement of the Asian prints. Press the seam allowances toward the Asian print squares.

4. Join the rows from step 2 and the rows from step 3 to make a block. Make nine blocks.

Make 9.

Quilt-Top Assembly

1. Join three blocks alternating with two 1" x 18½" green sashing strips to make a row. Press the seam allowances toward the sashing. Make three rows.

Make 3.

2. Sew the remaining bright green strips together end to end. Crosscut into four pieces, 1" x 55½", and two pieces, 1" x 56½".

3. Join the three rows, alternating them with two 1" x 55½" sashing pieces. Press the seam allowances toward the sashing.

4. Sew the two remaining 1" x 55½" sashing pieces to opposite sides of the quilt top. Sew the 1" x 56½" sashing pieces to the top and bottom edges of the quilt top.

5. Referring to "Adding Borders" on page 13, attach the border.

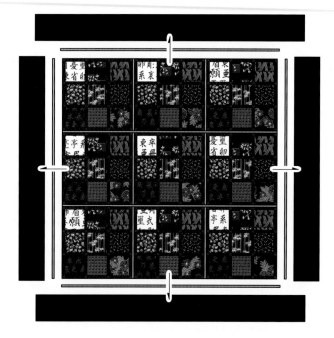

6. Layer the quilt top with batting and backing, and quilt as desired.

7. Referring to "Binding" on page 14, bind the edges of the quilt.

Black & White

I've always wanted to make a black-and-white quilt, but I couldn't resist adding a little punch of color with the bright green in the border!

Finished Quilt: 70½" x 70½"
Finished Block: 9½" x 9½"

Materials

Yardage is based on 42"-wide fabric.

2⅝ yards of black floral for blocks and border 4

2¼ yards of white floral for blocks and setting triangles

⅝ yard of black dot fabric for borders 1 and 3

⅓ yard of bright green fabric for border 2

⅝ yard of fabric for binding

4½ yards of fabric for backing

77" x 77" piece of batting

Cutting

From the black floral, cut:
2 strips, 7" x 42"; crosscut into 9 squares, 7" x 7"

15 strips, 2" x 42"; crosscut into:
- 32 rectangles, 2" x 7"
- 32 rectangles, 2" x 8½"
- 18 squares, 2" x 2"

7 strips, 6" x 42"

From the white floral, cut:
4 strips, 7" x 42"; crosscut into 16 squares, 7" x 7"

9 strips, 2" x 42"; crosscut into:
- 18 rectangles, 2" x 7"
- 18 rectangles, 2" x 8½"
- 32 squares, 2" x 2"

2 strips, 15" x 42"; crosscut into 3 squares, 15" x 15". Cut the squares twice diagonally to make 12 triangles.

2 squares, 7⅝" x 7⅝"; cut the squares once diagonally to make 4 triangles

From the black dot fabric, cut:
12 strips, 1½" x 42"

From the bright green fabric, cut:
6 strips, 1¼" x 42"

From the binding fabric, cut:
8 strips, 2¼" x 42"

Making the Blocks

1. To make block 1, sew 2" x 7" black floral rectangles to opposite sides of each 7" white floral square. Press the seam allowances toward the rectangles. Make 16.

Make 16.

2. Sew a 2" white square to each 2" x 8½" black rectangle. Press the seam allowances toward the rectangles.

Make 32.

Pieced and quilted by Sara Diepersloot

3. Sew the units from steps 1 and 2 together to complete the blocks. Press the seam allowances toward the black floral. Make 16 blocks.

Block 1.
Make 16.

4. Repeat steps 1–3 to make block 2, using the black floral squares and white floral rectangles. Make nine blocks.

Block 2.
Make 9.

Quilt-Top Assembly

1. Join the blocks and setting triangles into diagonal rows. Sew the rows together. Refer to "Making Diagonally Set Quilts" on page 12 to trim and square up the quilt top.

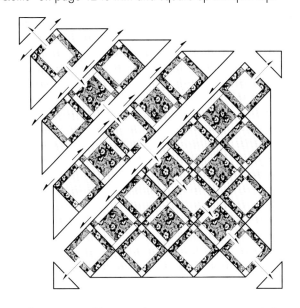

2. Referring to "Adding Borders" on page 13, attach the four rounds of borders.

3. Layer the quilt top with batting and backing, and quilt as desired.

4. Referring to "Binding" on page 14, bind the edges of the quilt.

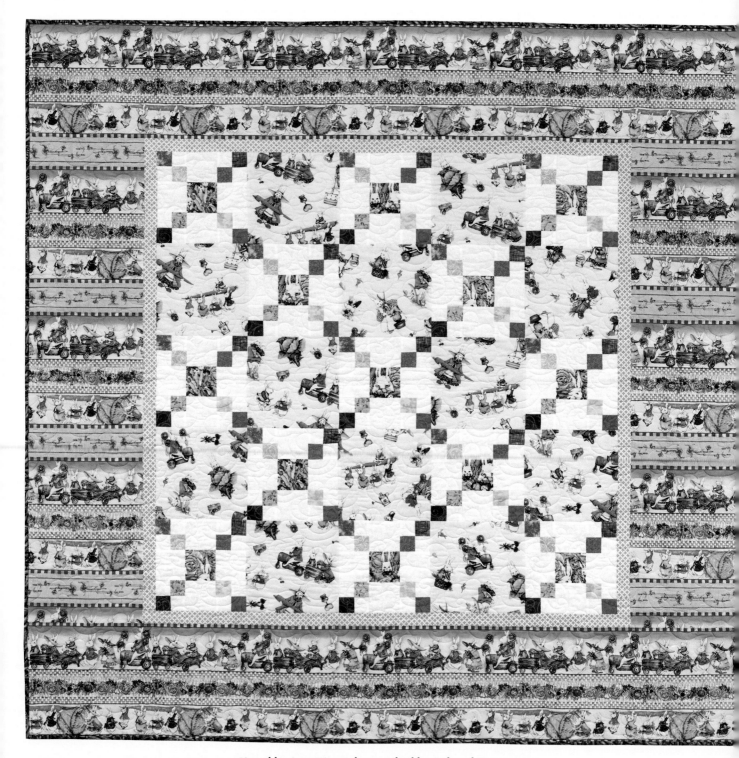

Pieced by Sara Diepersloot, quilted by Deborah Rasmussen

Bunnies in My Garden

Sometimes you find a whimsical fabric that's just too fun to cut up! A great solution is to use the fabric for setting squares, as I did in this quilt. I pulled colors from the fabric to make the blocks, and then I added a coordinating print that provided the little bunnies peeking out from the block centers.

Finished Quilt: 71" x 71"
Finished Block: 9" x 9"

Materials

Yardage is based on 42"-wide fabric.

3½ yards of bunny-striped fabric for outer border

1⅛ yards of white fabric for blocks

1 yard of bunny print 1 for setting squares

⅛ yard *each* of 8 different colored fabrics for blocks

⅓ yard of yellow checked fabric for inner border

¼ yard of bunny print 2 for blocks*

⅝ yard of fabric for binding

4½ yards of fabric for backing

77" x 77" piece of batting

Allow more if fussy cutting.

Cutting

From the white fabric, cut:
8 strips, 2" x 42"

5 strips, 3½" x 42"; crosscut into 52 squares, 3½" x 3½"

From *each* of the 8 different colored fabrics, cut:
1 strip, 2" x 42"

From bunny print 2, cut:
2 strips, 3½" x 42"; crosscut into 13 squares, 3½" x 3½"

From bunny print 1, cut:
3 strips, 9½" x 42"; crosscut into 12 squares, 9½" x 9½"

From the yellow checked fabric, cut:
5 strips, 1¾" x 42"

From the bunny-striped fabric, cut:
2 strips, 12" x 73", from the *lengthwise* grain

3 strips, 12" x 42", from the *crosswise* grain

From the binding fabric, cut:
8 strips, 2¼" x 42"

Making the Blocks

1. Sew a 2"-wide white strip to *each* of the eight colored strips. Press the seam allowances toward the colored strips. Crosscut each strip set into 13 segments, 2" wide.

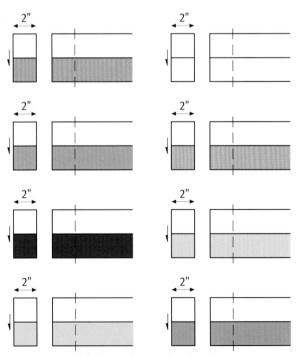

Make 1 strip set of each color.
Cut 13 segments from each.

2. Arrange eight different segments from step 1 into four pairs. Sew the pairs together to make four four-patch units. Make 13 four-patch units from each color combination, for a total of 52 four-patch units.

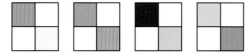

Make 13 of each.

3. Join two four-patch units and a white square as shown to make the top and bottom rows of the block. Join two white squares and a square of bunny print 2 to make the middle row of the block. Sew the rows together. Make 13 blocks.

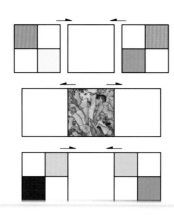

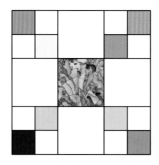

Make 13.

Quilt-Top Assembly

1. Arrange the pieced blocks and setting squares in rows as shown in the quilt diagram. Join the blocks into rows. Press the seam allowances toward the setting squares. Sew the rows together. Press.

2. Referring to "Adding Borders" on page 13, attach the inner and outer borders.

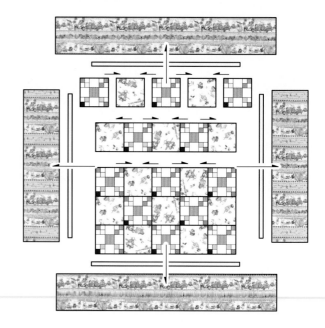

3. Layer the quilt top with batting and backing, and quilt as desired.

4. Referring to "Binding" on page 14, bind the edges of the quilt.

Surf's Up, Baby!

This fun baby quilt sews up quickly and makes a great gift. You can replace the theme fabric with any fun juvenile or novelty print and coordinate it with the baby's room.

Finished Quilt: 44" x 44"
Finished Block: 12" x 12"

Materials

Yardage is based on 42"-wide fabric.

⅝ yard of blue-and-green Hawaiian print for outer border

¼ yard of blue print for inner border

9 tropical print rectangles, 10" x 14", for blocks*

27 squares, 6" x 6", for blocks*

½ yard of fabric for binding

2⅞ yards of fabric for backing

50" x 50" piece of batting

I used about 20 different fabrics for the blocks in my quilt, but you can easily use more or fewer than that. You will need scraps to cut a total of 9 rectangles, 8½" x 12½", and 27 squares, 4½" x 4½".

Cutting

From the rectangles, cut:
9 rectangles, 8½" x 12½"

From the squares, cut:
27 squares, 4½" x 4½"

From the blue print, cut:
4 strips, 1½" x 42"

From the blue-and-green Hawaiian print, cut:
5 strips, 3¼" x 42"

From the binding fabric, cut:
5 strips, 2¼" x 42"

Making the Blocks

I suggest using a design wall when making this quilt. (See "Making a Design Wall" on page 13.) After cutting the fabrics, I like to arrange the rectangles and squares together, deciding which ones look best next to each other, until I am happy with the layout. Then I take down one block at a time from the design wall and assemble it. Refer to the quilt diagram on page 35 and audition your cut fabrics together before sewing.

1. Sew three 4½" squares together. Press seam allowances in one direction. Sew this unit to an 8½" x 12½" rectangle and press.

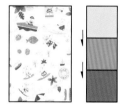

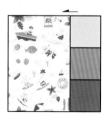

2. Repeat to make nine blocks.

Pieced and quilted by Sara Diepersloot

Quilt-Top Assembly

1. Following the quilt diagram, join the blocks in three rows of three blocks each. Press the seam allowances in the opposite direction from row to row. Sew the rows together. Press.

2. Referring to "Adding Borders" on page 13, attach the inner and outer borders.

3. Layer the quilt top with batting and backing, and quilt as desired.

4. Referring to "Binding" on page 14, bind the edges of the quilt.

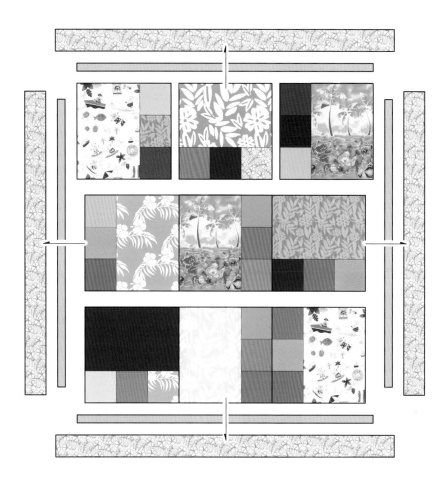

Pieced and quilted by Sara Diepersloot

Summertime

I made this quilt in the cold days of January, and the cheery colors made me think of sunny days and lemonade.

Finished Quilt: 58½" x 70½"
Finished Block: 11" x 11"

Materials

Yardage is based on 42"-wide fabric.

1⅓ yards of blue-and-yellow striped fabric for blocks

1⅛ yards of yellow-and-blue print for border

⅞ yard of blue fabric for sashing

⅜ yard *each* of 2 blue fabrics for blocks

⅜ yard *each* of 2 yellow fabrics for blocks

¼ yard *each* of 2 white fabrics for blocks

⅝ yard of fabric for binding

3¾ yards of fabric for backing

65" x 77" piece of batting

Cutting

From *each* of the 2 blue and 2 yellow fabrics for blocks, cut:
3 strips, 3¼" x 42"; crosscut into:
    10 squares, 3¼" x 3¼" (20 total)
    10 rectangles, 3¼" x 6" (20 total)

From *each* of the 2 white fabrics, cut:
2 strips, 3¼" x 42"; crosscut into 20 squares,
3¼" x 3¼" (40 total)

From the blue-and-yellow striped fabric, cut:
7 strips, 6" x 42"; crosscut into 40 squares, 6" x 6"

From the blue fabric for sashing, cut:
16 strips, 1½" x 42"; crosscut 5 strips into 15 pieces,
1½" x 11½"

From the yellow-and-blue print, cut:
7 strips, 5" x 42"

From the binding fabric, cut:
7 strips, 2¼" x 42"

Making the Blocks

You will be making two different blocks, using one blue, one yellow, and one white for each block. Choose which fabrics you want to go together, and label them block A and block B. The stripe is the same in both blocks.

1. Sew a blue square to a white square. Press the seam allowances toward the blue. Sew this unit to a blue rectangle. Press the seam allowances toward the blue. Repeat with a yellow square, a white square, and a yellow rectangle.

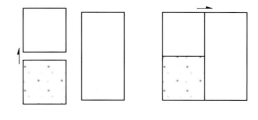

2. Using the blue unit, the yellow unit, and two striped squares, assemble the block as shown. Make 10 *each* of block A and block B, for a total of 20 blocks.

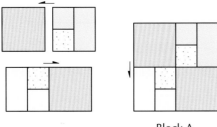

Block A.
Make 10.

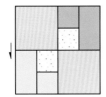

Block B.
Make 10.

Quilt-Top Assembly

1. Lay out the blocks in five rows of four blocks each, alternating blocks A and B as shown. Sew the blocks together, alternating them with 1½" x 11½" sashing pieces, to make the rows. Press all seam allowances toward the sashing.

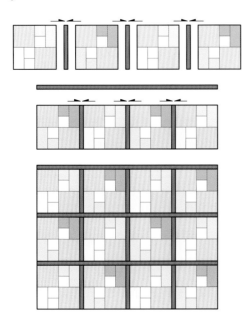

2. Sew the remaining blue strips together end to end. Crosscut into four pieces, 1½" x 47½"; two pieces, 1½" x 49½"; and two pieces, 1½" x 59½".

3. Join the rows, alternating them with the 1½" x 47½" sashing pieces.

4. Sew the 1½" x 59½" sashing pieces to the sides of the quilt top.

5. Sew the 1½" x 49½" sashing pieces to the top and bottom edges of the quilt top.

6. Referring to "Adding Borders" on page 13, attach the border.

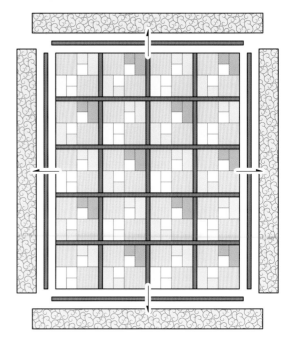

7. Layer the quilt top with batting and backing, and quilt as desired.

8. Referring to "Binding" on page 14, bind the edges of the quilt.

Pineapple Paradise

Our family loves to go to Maui, and this pineapple fabric reminds me of those wonderful trips. I backed the quilt with a fabulous brown-and-black Hawaiian print to finish off the theme. Aloha!

Finished Quilt: 56½" x 76½"
Finished Pineapple Block: 10½" x 10½"
Finished Pinwheel Block: 3½" x 3½"

Materials

Yardage is based on 42"-wide fabric.

1¾ yards of pineapple print for blocks and outer border

1⅝ yards of green print for Pinwheels and setting triangles

1 yard of green bamboo print for sashing

1 yard of gold batik for blocks and inner border

⅓ yard of tan print for Pinwheels

¼ yard of ivory batik for blocks

⅝ yard of fabric for binding

4⅝ yards of fabric for backing

63" x 83" piece of batting

Cutting

From the pineapple print, cut:
2 strips, 8" x 42"; crosscut into 8 squares, 8" x 8"

7 strips, 5" x 42"

From the gold batik, cut:
7 strips, 2" x 42"; crosscut into 32 rectangles, 2" x 8"

7 strips, 1¾" x 42"

From the ivory batik, cut:
2 strips, 2" x 42"; crosscut into 32 squares, 2" x 2"

From the tan print, cut:
3 strips, 3" x 42"; crosscut into 34 squares, 3" x 3". Cut the squares once diagonally to make 68 triangles.

From the green print, cut:
3 strips, 3" x 42"; crosscut into 34 squares, 3" x 3". Cut the squares once diagonally to make 68 triangles.

2 squares, 21¼" x 21¼"; cut the squares twice diagonally to make 8 side setting triangles (2 are extra)

2 squares, 13½" x 13½"; cut the squares once diagonally to make 4 corner setting triangles

From the green bamboo print, cut:
8 strips, 4" x 42"; crosscut into 24 rectangles, 4" x 11"

From the binding fabric, cut:
7 strips, 2¼" x 42"

Making the Blocks

1. Sew gold batik rectangles to opposite sides of a pineapple print square. Press the seam allowances toward the gold. Make eight.

Make 8.

2. Sew an ivory batik square to each end of one of the remaining gold batik rectangles. Press the seam allowances toward the gold. Make 16.

Make 16.

Pieced and quilted by Sara Diepersloot

3. Join the units from steps 1 and 2 to make a block. Press the seam allowances toward the pineapple print. Make eight Pineapple blocks.

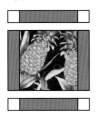 

Make 8.

4. Using the triangles cut from 3" squares, sew the green triangles and the tan triangles together into pairs. Press the seam allowances toward the green. Make 68.

Make 68.

5. Join four units from step 4 to make a Pinwheel block, rotating the triangles as shown. Make 17. Square up to 4" x 4".

Make 17.

Quilt-Top Assembly

Each row in this quilt is slightly different. Using the blocks, the Pinwheels, and the green bamboo print sashing pieces, join into rows as directed.

1. To make row 1, sew sashing pieces to opposite sides of one block. Press the seam allowances toward the sashing. Sew a Pinwheel to each end of a sashing piece. Press the seam allowances toward the sashing. Sew the Pinwheel unit to the top edge of the block, and then sew a side setting triangle cut from the 21¼" squares to each end of the row.

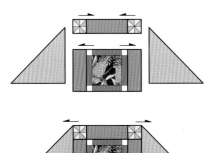

Row 1

2. To make row 2, sew four Pinwheels and three sashing pieces together into a unit. Press the seam allowances toward the sashing. Sew four sashing pieces and three blocks together into a unit. Press the seam allowances toward the sashing. Sew five Pinwheels and four sashing pieces together into a unit. Join the unit with four Pinwheels to the block unit. Sew a side setting triangle to the left end of the row. Join to the unit with five Pinwheels.

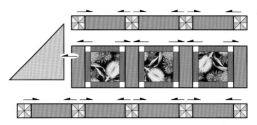

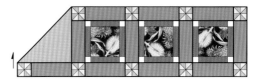

Row 2

3. To make row 3, sew four sashing pieces and three blocks together into a unit. Press the seam allowances toward the sashing. Sew four Pinwheels and three sashing pieces together into a unit. Press the seam allowances toward the sashing. Join the block unit to the Pinwheel unit. Sew a side setting triangle to the right end of the row.

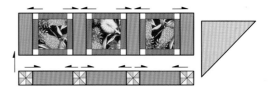

Row 3

4. To make row 4, sew sashing pieces to opposite sides of the remaining block. Press the seam allowances toward the sashing. Sew a Pinwheel to each end of a sashing piece. Press the seam allowances toward the sashing. Sew the Pinwheel unit to the bottom edge of the block, and then sew a side setting triangle to each end of the row.

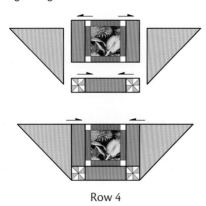

Row 4

5. Sew the rows together. Add a corner setting triangle cut from the 13½" squares to each corner of the quilt.

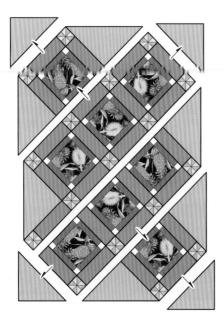

6. Referring to "Making Diagonally Set Quilts" on page 12, square up your quilt top.

7. Referring to "Adding Borders" on page 13, attach the inner and outer borders.

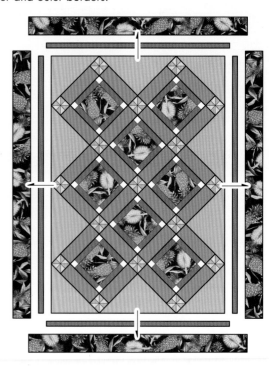

8. Layer the quilt top with batting and backing, and quilt as desired.

9. Referring to "Binding" on page 14, bind the edges of the quilt.

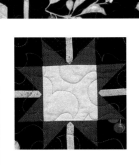

Cherry Blossoms

This beautiful black print was a tablecloth in its first life. I fell in love with the colors so instantly that I promptly brought it home and began to cut it up for a quilt. I guess that's when you know you really are addicted to quilting!

Finished Quilt: 72½" x 72½"

Materials

Yardage is based on 42"-wide fabric.

3¾ yards of black cherry-blossom print for blocks

1⅔ yards of black dot fabric for sashing

¾ yard of red fabric for star points

½ yard of green fabric for sashing

⅓ yard of yellow fabric for star centers

⅝ yard of fabric for binding

4⅓ yards of fabric for backing

79" x 79" piece of batting

Cutting

From the black dot fabric, cut:
24 strips, 2¼" x 42"

From the green fabric, cut:
12 strips, 1" x 42"

From the red fabric, cut:
8 strips, 2½" x 42"; crosscut into 128 squares, 2½" x 2½"

From the black cherry-blossom print, cut:
5 strips, 16½" x 42"; crosscut into 9 squares, 16½" x 16½"

8 strips, 4½" x 42"; crosscut into 20 squares, 4½" x 4½", and 12 rectangles, 4½" x 16½"

From the yellow fabric, cut:
2 strips, 4½" x 42"; crosscut into 16 squares, 4½" x 4½"

From the binding fabric, cut:
8 strips, 2¼" x 42"

Making the Units

1. Sew a black sashing strip, a green sashing strip, and another black sashing strip together to make a strip set. Make 12 strip sets. Press the seam allowances toward the black. Cut each strip set into two segments, 4½" x 16½", for a total of 24 segments.

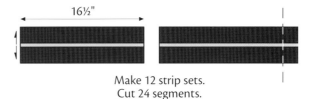

16½"

Make 12 strip sets.
Cut 24 segments.

2. Mark a diagonal line on the wrong side of each red square. Lay a red square on the end of a segment from step 1, right sides together, and sew on the diagonal line as shown. Trim off the excess about ¼" from the sewn line. Press the seam allowances toward the red star point.

3. Repeat step 2 to add a red star point to each corner. Make 24 sashing units.

Make 24.

4. Using the remaining red squares, add red triangles to two corners of a 4½" cherry-blossom square as shown to make star points for the borders. Make 16 star-point units.

Make 16.

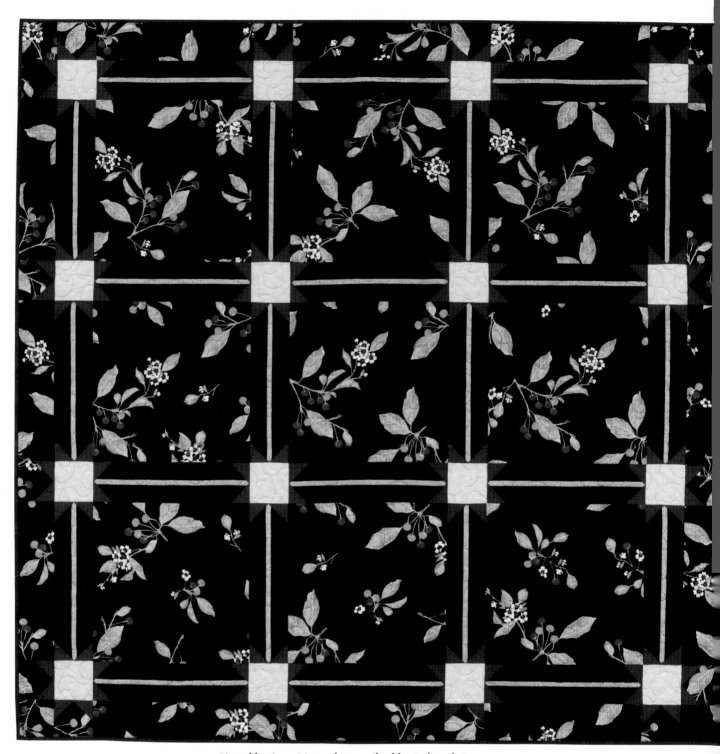

Pieced by Sara Diepersloot, quilted by Deborah Rasmussen

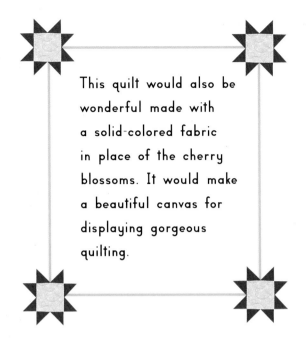

This quilt would also be wonderful made with a solid-colored fabric in place of the cherry blossoms. It would make a beautiful canvas for displaying gorgeous quilting.

Quilt-Top Assembly

The quilt top consists of three different rows.

1. For row 1, join two of the remaining 4½" cherry-blossom squares, four star-point units from step 4 above, and three 4½" x 16½" cherry-blossom rectangles as shown. Press the seam allowances toward the cherry-blossom print. Make two rows.

Row 1
Make 2.

2. For row 2, join two star-point units, four yellow squares, and three sashing units as shown. Press the seam allowances toward the yellow squares. Make four rows.

Row 2.
Make 4.

3. For row 3, join two 4½" x 16½" cherry-blossom rectangles, four sashing units, and three 16½" cherry-blossom squares. Press the seam allowances toward the cherry-blossom print. Make three rows.

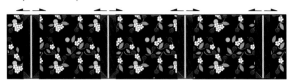

Row 3.
Make 3.

4. Join the rows as shown. Press.

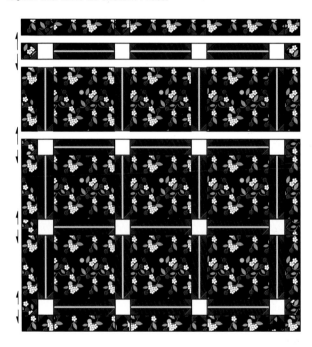

5. Layer the quilt top with batting and backing, and quilt as desired.

6. Referring to "Binding" on page 14, bind the edges of the quilt.

Pieced and quilted by Sara Diepersloot

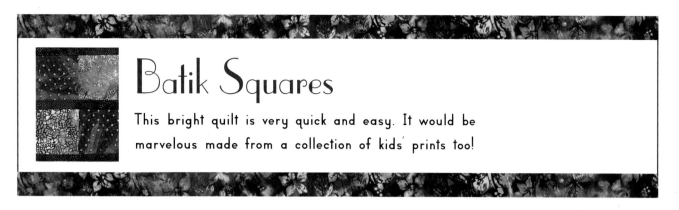

Batik Squares

This bright quilt is very quick and easy. It would be marvelous made from a collection of kids' prints too!

Finished Quilt: 57½" x 66½"

Materials

Yardage is based on 42"-wide fabric.

⅜ yard *each* of 10 different batik fabrics for blocks

1⅛ yards of multicolored batik fabric for outer border

½ yard of blue dot batik fabric for sashing

⅓ yard of blue batik fabric for inner border

⅝ yard of fabric for binding

3¾ yards of fabric for backing

64" x 73" piece of batting

Cutting

From *each* of the 10 different batik fabrics, cut:
2 strips, 5" x 42"; crosscut into 10 squares, 5" x 5"

From the blue dot batik fabric, cut:
10 strips, 1½" x 42"

From the blue batik fabric, cut:
6 strips, 1½" x 42"

From the multicolored batik fabric, cut:
6 strips, 5½" x 42"

From the binding fabric, cut:
7 strips, 2¼" x 42"

Quilt-Top Assembly

1. Before you begin, decide on the placement of your fabrics. Using one square of each of the 10 different batik fabrics, place them in the order you would like from left to right for the first row. In each consecutive row, keep the fabrics in the same order, but shift them one position to the right, moving the last square on the right so that it appears on the left end of the next row.

2. Sew 10 batik squares together to make a row. Press the seam allowances in one direction. Make 10 rows, paying close attention to the placement of fabrics in each row, and pressing the seam allowances in the opposite direction from row to row.

3. Sew the blue dot sashing strips together end to end and cut nine strips, 1½" x 45½". Sew the block rows together, alternating them with the sashing strips. Press the seam allowances toward the sashing.

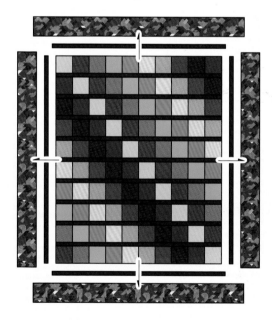

4. Referring to "Adding Borders" on page 13, attach the inner and outer borders.

5. Layer the quilt top with batting and backing, and quilt as desired.

6. Referring to "Binding" on page 14, bind the edges of the quilt.

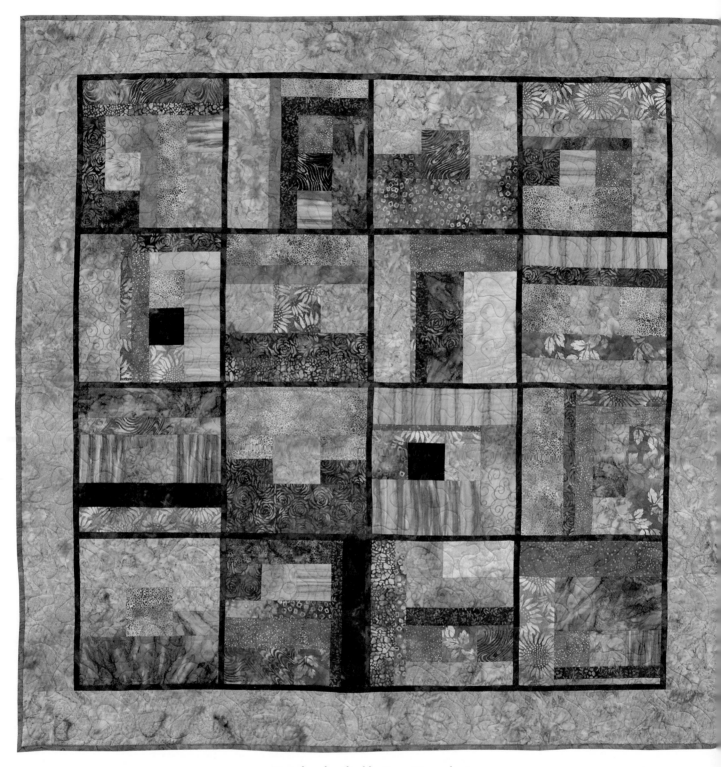

Pieced and quilted by Sara Diepersloot

Batik Addiction

Do you have a huge stash of those yummy batiks like I do? This is the perfect way to showcase them and use them up so that you can go out and buy more!

Finished Quilt: 60" x 60"
Finished Block: 12" x 12"

Materials

Yardage is based on 42"-wide fabric.

Scraps of batik fabrics to total 2⅞ yards*

1 yard of blue-and-green batik fabric for border

½ yard of purple batik fabric for sashing

⅝ yard of fabric for binding

3¾ yards of fabric for backing

66" x 66" piece of batting

I used about 25 different batiks for the blocks in my quilt. You will need scraps in all different sizes from 1" strips to 4" x 12½" pieces, as well as some 5"-wide pieces. Fat eighths, fat quarters, and ¼-yard cuts work well if you don't have enough scraps.

Cutting

For this quilt, I suggest cutting and piecing one block at a time.

Cutting for one of block 1 (make 3)

From batik scraps, cut:
2 rectangles, 4½" x 12½"
4 rectangles, 2½" x 4½"
1 square, 4½" x 4½"

Cutting for one of block 2 (make 3)

From batik scraps, cut:
3 squares, 4½" x 4½"
2 rectangles, 2½" x 12½"
1 rectangle, 2" x 12½"
1 rectangle, 3" x 12½"

Cutting for one of block 3 (make 3)

From batik scraps, cut:
4 squares, 3½" x 3½"
1 rectangle, 2" x 9½"
1 rectangle, 3" x 9½"
1 rectangle, 3½" x 6½"
1 rectangle, 2½" x 9½"
1 rectangle, 2½" x 12½"
1 rectangle, 1½" x 12½"

Cutting for one of block 4 (make 3)

From batik scraps, cut:
1 rectangle, 1½" x 12½"
3 squares, 3½" x 3½"
1 rectangle, 4" x 12½"
1 rectangle, 2" x 11"
1 rectangle, 2" x 6½"
1 rectangle, 2" x 8"
1 rectangle, 3½" x 9½"

Cutting for one of block 5 (make 3)

From batik scraps, cut:
3 squares, 3½" x 3½"
1 rectangle, 3½" x 9½"
1 rectangle, 1½" x 9½"
1 rectangle, 1" x 9½"
1 rectangle, 3½" x 12½"
1 rectangle, 5" x 9½"

Cutting for one of block 6 (make 1)

From batik scraps, cut:
3 squares, 3½" x 3½"
1 rectangle, 3½" x 9½"
1 rectangle, 1½" x 9½"
1 rectangle, 1" x 9½"
1 rectangle, 3½" x 12½"
1 rectangle, 5" x 9½"

Cutting sashing and borders

From the purple batik fabric, cut:
13 strips, 1" x 42"; crosscut 4 strips into 12 pieces,
1" x 12½"

From the blue-and-green batik fabric, cut:
6 strips, 5" x 42"

From the binding fabric, cut:
7 strips, 2¼" x 42"

Making the Blocks

Follow the block diagrams to make the blocks. Press
the seam allowances as indicated by the arrows in the
diagrams.

1. Block 1. Join the pieces for one block as shown; press.
Make a total of three blocks.

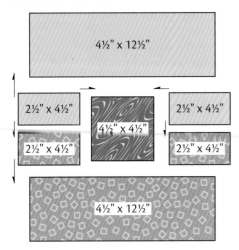

Make 3.

2. Block 2. Join the pieces for one block as shown; press.
Make a total of three blocks.

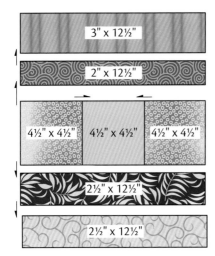

Make 3.

3. Block 3. Join the pieces for one block as shown; press.
Make a total of three blocks.

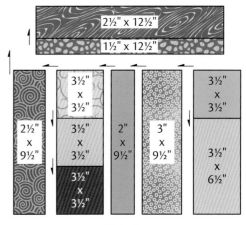

Make 3.

4. Block 4. Join the pieces for one block as shown; press.
Make a total of three blocks.

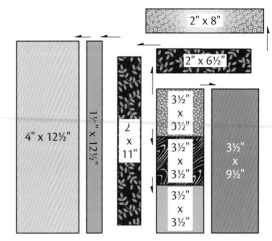

Make 3.

5. Block 5. Join the pieces for one block as shown; press.
Make a total of three blocks.

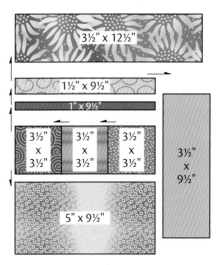

Make 3.

6. Block 6. Join the pieces for one block as shown; press. Make just one of these blocks.

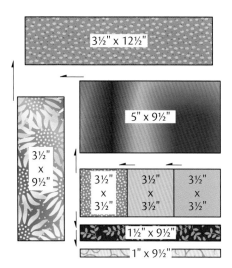

Make 1.

Quilt-Top Assembly

1. Experiment with the arrangement of the blocks until you are pleased with the design. You may follow the row diagrams below, or come up with your own configuration. Play around with the orientation of your blocks as well. For example, there are three of block 3, but I turned them in different directions within the quilt top. Join the blocks into rows, alternating them with the 1" x 12½" sashing pieces.

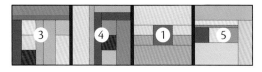

Row 1

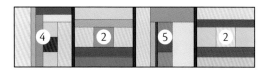

Row 2

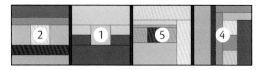

Row 3

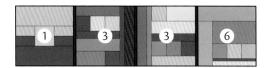

Row 4

2. Sew the remaining purple batik strips together end to end. Crosscut into five pieces, 1" x 50", and two pieces, 1" x 51".

3. Sew the rows together, alternating them with 1" x 50" sashing pieces. Sew the remaining 1" x 50" sashing pieces to the sides of the quilt top. Sew the 1" x 51" sashing pieces to the top and bottom edges of the quilt top.

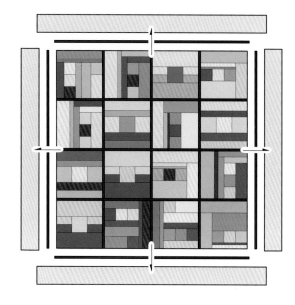

4. Referring to "Adding Borders" on page 13, attach the border.

5. Layer the quilt top with batting and backing, and quilt as desired.

6. Referring to "Binding" on page 14, bind the edges of the quilt.

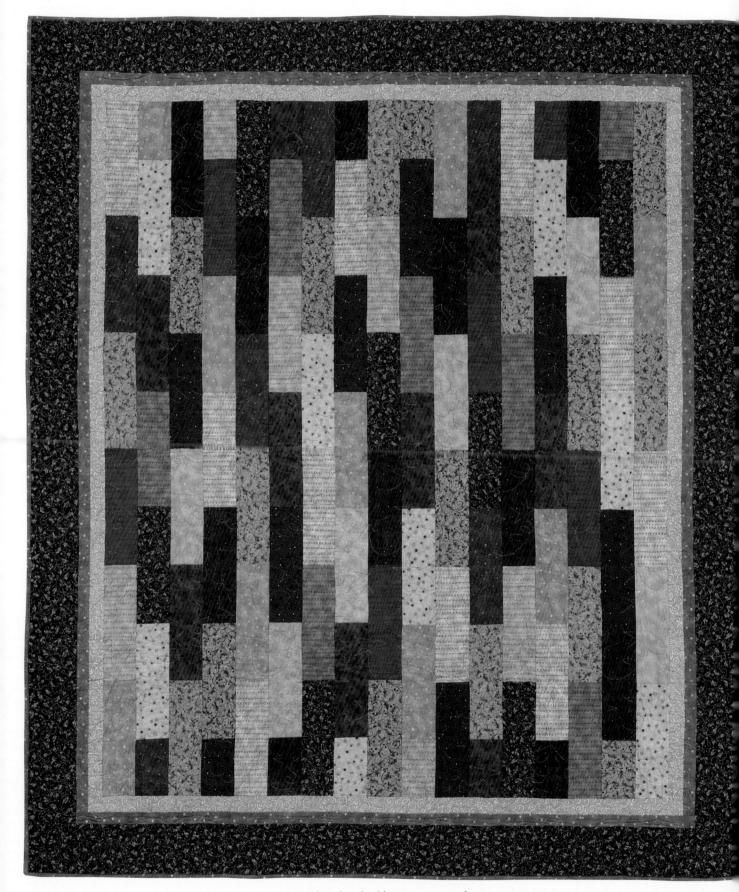

Pieced and quilted by Sara Diepersloot

Quick Bricks

Fat quarters are so irresistible. Grab a bundle of your favorites and go!

Finished Quilt: 59" x 69"

Materials

Yardage is based on 42"-wide fabric.

14 fat quarters of orange, red, blue, and green prints for blocks

1 yard of red print for outer border

⅜ yard of orange print for inner border

⅓ yard of green print for middle border

⅝ yard of fabric for binding

3¾ yards of fabric for backing

65" x 75" piece of batting

Cutting

Be sure to cut across the 21" length of the fat quarter.

From *each* of the 14 fat quarters, cut:
4 strips, 3¼" x 21"; crosscut into 8 rectangles, 3¼" x 10" (112 total; 2 are extra)

From the orange print, cut:
6 strips, 1¾" x 42"

From the green print, cut:
6 strips, 1½" x 42"

From the red print, cut:
7 strips, 4" x 42"

From the binding fabric, cut:
7 strips, 2¼" x 42"

Quilt-Top Assembly

I used a design wall to help me lay out my quilt. (See "Making a Design Wall" on page 13.) You can also use the floor, or a large table. I spent a bit of time just laying out the "bricks," or rectangles, playing with the placement of the fabrics until the design was pleasing to my eye. I tried to space the colors and different fabrics evenly throughout the quilt.

You will make two different vertical rows, one with six rectangles and one with seven. They will alternate in the quilt layout. Note that you will have two extra rectangles.

1. To make row 1, sew together six rectangles end to end. Make nine rows; press all the seam allowances in the same direction.

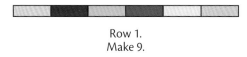

Row 1.
Make 9.

2. To make row 2, sew together seven rectangles end to end. Make eight rows; press all the seam allowances in the same direction.

Row 2.
Make 8.

3. Trim the first and last rectangle in each row 2, measuring 5" from the seam line as shown. Now each row 2 should be the same length as row 1.

Trim.   Trim.
↓ 5"   ↓ 5"

4. Alternating rows 1 and 2, sew the rows together to complete the quilt top.

5. Referring to "Adding Borders" on page 13, attach the inner, middle, and outer borders.

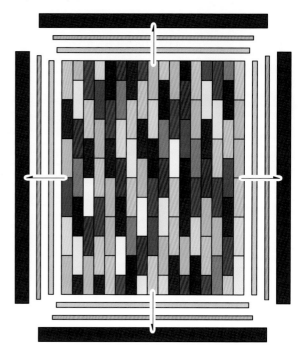

6. Layer the quilt top with batting and backing, and quilt as desired.

7. Referring to "Binding" on page 14, bind the edges of the quilt.

Many of the fabrics in this quilt were part of a holiday collection, but the color scheme lends itself to using the quilt anytime of the year. When you are shopping for fabrics, don't pass right by holiday prints—you might find just what you are looking for!

Christmas Stars

The star blocks in this quilt offer the ideal location for spotlighting two of your favorite prints in the center squares.

Finished Quilt: 71½" x 71½"
Finished Block: 20" x 20"

Materials

Yardage is based on 42"-wide fabric.

2⅞ yards of cream fabric for background

⅛ yard *each* of 16 different fabrics for blocks*

1⅛ yards of green fabric for star points

1 yard of red fabric for star points

1 yard of dark green fabric for border

¾ yard of green fabric for sashing

¼ yard *each* of 2 novelty prints for blocks

⅝ yard of fabric for binding

4¾ yards of fabric for backing

78" x 78" piece of batting

*Or 1 strip, 2½" x 25", each of 16 different fabrics.

Cutting

From *each of the 16 fabrics for blocks*, cut:
1 strip, 2½" x 42"

From *each of the 2 novelty prints*, cut:
1 strip, 6½" x 42"; crosscut 1 strip into 5 squares,
6½" x 6½", and the other strip into 4 squares, 6½" x 6½"

From the green fabric for star points, cut:
6 strips, 5½" x 42"; crosscut into 40 squares, 5½" x 5½"

From the cream fabric, cut:
12 strips, 5½" x 42"; crosscut each strip into:
    3 rectangles, 5½" x 10½" (36 total)
    1 square, 5½" x 5½" (12 total)
4 strips, 5½" x 42"; crosscut into 24 squares, 5½" x 5½"

From the red fabric, cut:
5 strips, 5½" x 42"; crosscut into 32 squares, 5½" x 5½"

From the green fabric for sashing, cut:
13 strips, 1½" x 42"; crosscut 3 strips into 6 sashing pieces,
1½" x 20½"

From the dark green fabric, cut:
7 strips, 4" x 42"

From the binding fabric, cut:
8 strips, 2¼" x 42"

Making the Blocks

1. Decide on the order in which you would like your 16 fabrics (the 2½" strips) positioned around the novelty-print square. You might want to make a numbered sketch on paper, and attach a scrap of fabric in each position; then number your fabrics 1 to 16. You will sew the strips together to make strip sets, and then cut them into segments.

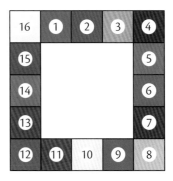

Pieced and quilted by Sara Diepersloot

2. Make strip sets of the numbered fabrics as shown in the diagrams. Press all the seam allowances in the same direction.

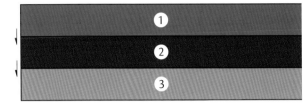

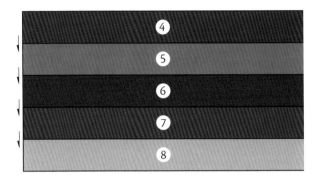

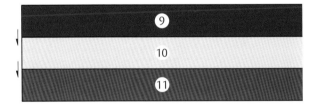

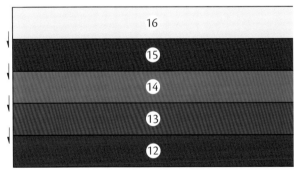

Make 1 of each.

3. Cut each of the strip sets into nine segments, 2½" wide.

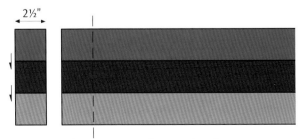

Cut 9 segments from each strip set.

4. Sew a 1-2-3 segment to the top edge and a 9-10-11 segment to the bottom edge of each 6½" novelty-print square. Press. Sew a 4-5-6-7-8 segment to the right side and a 12-13-14-15-16 segment to the left side of each square. Press.

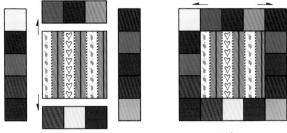

Make 9.

5. Mark a diagonal line from corner to corner on the wrong side of the 5½" green squares. Lay one square on a 5½" x 10½" cream rectangle, right sides together, and sew on the diagonal line. Trim off the excess about ¼" from the sewn line. Press the seam allowances toward the green star point. Repeat with a second green square on the other end of the rectangle, orienting the diagonal line in the opposite direction. Make 20 green star-point units.

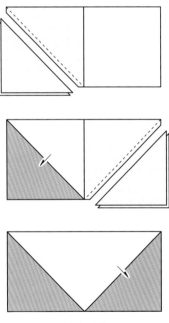

Make 20.

6. Repeat step 5 with the red squares and the remaining cream rectangles to make 16 red star-point units.

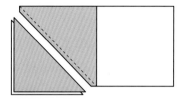

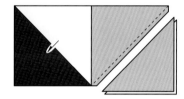

Make 16.

7. You will be making five blocks with green star points and four blocks with red star points. Decide which star-point fabric is going to be paired with which star-center fabric. Arrange the 5½" cream squares, the star-point units, and the center squares as shown. Join the units into rows, and then sew the rows together.

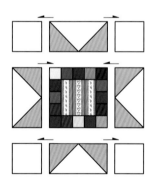

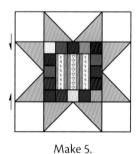

Make 5.

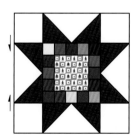

Make 4.

Quilt-Top Assembly

1. Sew the blocks and the 1½" x 20½" sashing pieces into rows as shown. Make two rows with green blocks on the ends and a red block in the center. Make one row with red blocks on the ends and a green block in the center. Press the seam allowances toward the sashing strips.

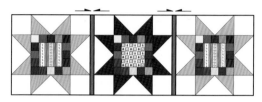

2. Sew the remaining green sashing strips together end to end. Crosscut into four pieces, 1½" x 62½", and two pieces, 1½" x 64½". Sew the 1½" x 62½" sashing pieces between the rows, and to the sides of the quilt top. Sew the 1½" x 64½" sashing pieces to the top and bottom edges of the quilt top.

3. Referring to "Adding Borders" on page 13, attach the border.

4. Layer the quilt top with batting and backing, and quilt as desired.

5. Referring to "Binding" on page 14, bind the edges of the quilt.

Hidden Stars

In addition to the more obvious stars, watch the "hidden" stars emerge when you piece this quilt together.

Finished Quilt: 73" x 89"

Materials

Yardage is based on 42"-wide fabric.

3¾ yards of gold print for blocks and background

2½ yards of gold-and-pink floral for blocks and outer border

1⅔ yards of light green print for blocks

⅔ yard of brown print for blocks

½ yard of pink print for blocks

½ yard of green dot fabric for inner border

¼ yard of brown dot fabric for sashing

⅔ yard of fabric for binding

5¾ yards of fabric for backing

79" x 95" piece of batting

Cutting

From the gold print, cut:
15 strips, 2½" x 42"; crosscut 8 strips into 120 squares, 2½" x 2½"

12 strips, 4½" x 42"; crosscut into 48 rectangles, 4½" x 8½"

7 strips, 3" x 42"; crosscut into 80 squares, 3" x 3". Cut the squares once diagonally to make 160 triangles.

4 strips, 1¾" x 42"

From the pink print, cut:
6 strips, 2½" x 42"; crosscut 3 strips into 40 squares, 2½" x 2½"

From the gold-and-pink floral, cut:
3 strips, 4½" x 42"; crosscut into 24 squares, 4½" x 4½"

9 strips, 7½" x 42"

From the light green print, cut:
12 strips, 4½" x 42"; crosscut into 96 squares, 4½" x 4½"

From the brown print, cut:
7 strips, 3" x 42"; crosscut into 80 squares, 3" x 3". Cut the squares once diagonally to make 160 triangles.

From the brown dot fabric, cut:
4 strips, 1¼" x 42"

From the green dot fabric, cut:
7 strips, 1¾" x 42"

From the binding fabric, cut:
9 strips, 2¼" x 42"

Making the Units

1. Sew 2½" pink strips and 2½" gold strips together in pairs to make three strip sets. Press the seam allowances toward the pink. Crosscut the strip sets into 48 segments, 2½" wide.

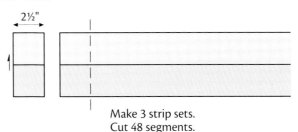

Make 3 strip sets.
Cut 48 segments.

2. Sew two 2½" segments together to make a four-patch unit. Make 24 units.

Make 24.

Pieced and quilted by Sara Diepersloot

3. Join two gold-and-pink floral squares and two four-patch units into a Double Four Patch block. Press the seam allowances toward the floral. Make 12 blocks.

Make 12.

4. Draw a diagonal line from corner to corner on the wrong side of the light green squares. Lay a square on one end of a 4½" x 8½" gold rectangle, right sides together. Sew on the drawn line. Trim off the excess, ¼" from the stitching line. Press the seam allowances toward the triangle. Repeat on the other end of the rectangle, orienting the diagonal line in the opposite direction. Make 48 of these star-point units.

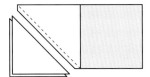 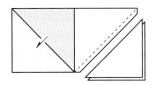

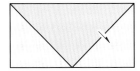

Make 48.

5. Sew the gold triangles and the brown triangles into pairs as shown. Press the seam allowances toward the brown. Square up the units to 2½" x 2½". Make 160.

Make 160.

6. Join two triangle-square units from step 5 and two 2½" gold squares to make a unit as shown. Make 40.

Make 40.

7. Join two triangle-square units from step 5, one gold square, and one pink square as shown. Make 40.

Make 40.

8. Join one 1¾" x 42" gold strip, one 1¼" x 42" brown dot strip, and one 2½" x 42" gold strip to make a strip set. Make four strip sets. Crosscut into 14 segments, 8½" wide.

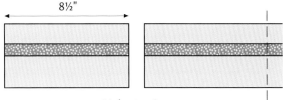

Make 4 strip sets.
Cut 14 segments.

Quilt-Top Assembly

1. Arrange the triangle-square units, the star-point units, the Double Four Patch blocks, and the strip-set segments as shown. Join the units into rows. Press each row away from the green star points. Sew the rows together.

2. Referring to "Adding Borders" on page 13, attach the inner and outer borders.

3. Layer the quilt top with batting and backing, and quilt as desired.

4. Referring to "Binding" on page 14, bind the edges of the quilt.

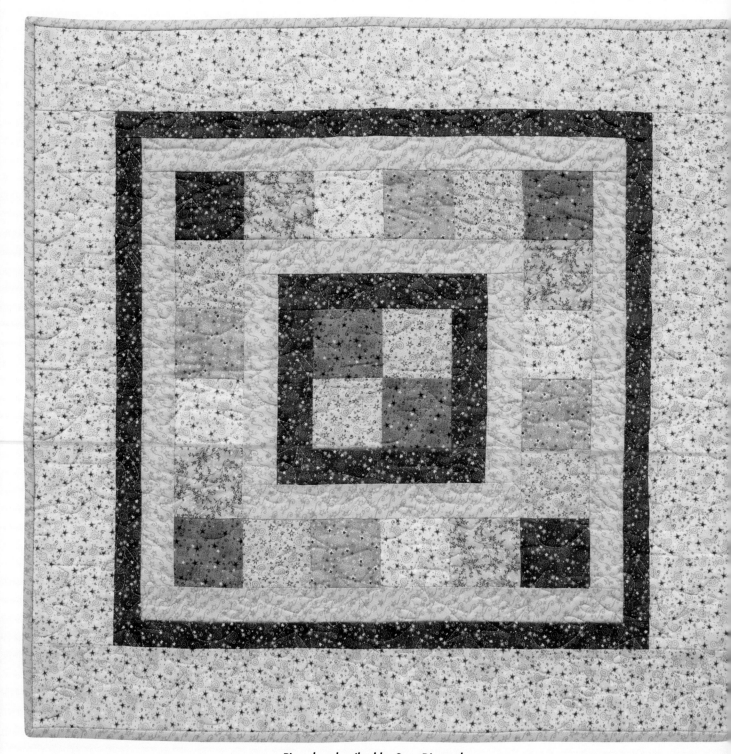

Pieced and quilted by Sara Diepersloot

Squares Around

This sweet and easy quilt is the perfect size to use as a decorative table topper or as a welcoming wall hanging.

Finished Quilt: 26" x 26"

Materials

Yardage is based on 42"-wide fabric.

½ yard of cream star print for border 6 and squares border

⅜ yard of brown print for borders 1 and 5, and squares border

¼ yard of cream print for borders 2 and 4

⅛ yard *each* of 2 different pink prints for squares border

⅛ yard of dark pink print for center four patch and squares border

⅛ yard of cream-and-pink print for center four patch and squares border

¼ yard of fabric for binding

1 yard of fabric for backing

32" x 32" piece of batting

Cutting

From the dark pink print, cut:
4 squares, 3" x 3"

From the cream-and-pink print, cut:
6 squares, 3" x 3"

From the brown print, cut:
1 strip, 1¾" x 42"; crosscut into:
    2 pieces, 1¾" x 5½"
    2 pieces, 1¾" x 8"
2 strips, 1½" x 42"; crosscut into:
    2 pieces, 1½" x 18"
    2 pieces, 1½" x 20"
2 squares, 3" x 3"

From the cream print, cut:
3 strips, 1¾" x 42"; crosscut into:
    2 pieces, 1¾" x 8"
    2 pieces, 1¾" x 10½"
    2 pieces, 1¾" x 15½"
    2 pieces, 1¾" x 18"

From *each* of the 2 different pink prints, cut:
4 squares, 3" x 3" (8 total)

From the cream star print, cut:
3 strips, 3½" x 42"; crosscut into:
    2 pieces, 3½" x 20"
    2 pieces, 3½" x 26"
4 squares, 3" x 3"

From the binding fabric, cut:
3 strips, 2¼" x 42"

Quilt-Top Assembly

1. Sew two dark pink squares and two cream-and-pink squares together to make a four-patch unit.

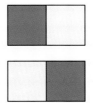

2. Sew the 1¾" x 5½" brown pieces to the sides of the four-patch unit. Press. Sew the 1¾" x 8" brown pieces to the top and bottom edges and press.

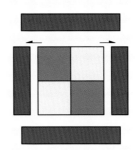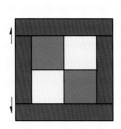

3. Sew the 1¾" x 8" cream pieces to the sides of the unit from step 2. Sew the 1¾" x 10½" cream pieces to the top and bottom edges. Press.

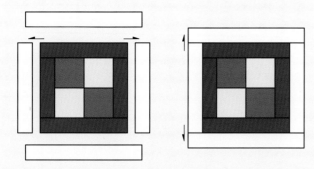

4. Join four assorted 3" squares; press. Make two rows and sew them to the two sides of the block. Join six assorted 3" squares and press. Make two rows and sew them to the top and bottom edges of the block. Press.

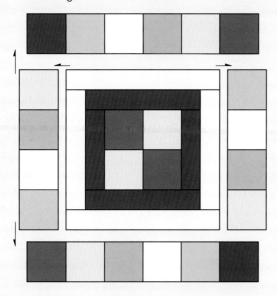

5. Sew the 1¾" x 15½" cream pieces to the sides of the block. Sew the 1¾" x 18" cream pieces to the top and bottom edges of the block. Press.

6. Sew the 1½" x 18" brown pieces to the sides of the block. Sew the 1½" x 20" brown pieces to the top and bottom edges of the block. Press.

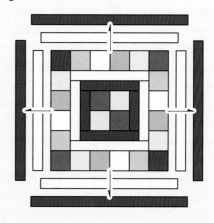

7. Sew the 3½" x 20" star print pieces to the sides of the block. Sew the 3½" x 26" star print pieces to the top and bottom edges of the block. Press.

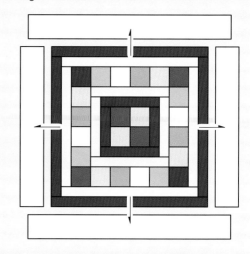

8. Layer the quilt top with batting and backing, and quilt as desired.

9. Referring to "Binding" on page 14, bind the edges of the quilt.

Simple Scrap Table Runner

Here's a great way to use those 2½" strips sold in jelly rolls or leftover strips and scraps from another project. This runner sews together in a snap!

Finished Table Runner: 25" x 45"

Materials

Yardage is based on 42"-wide fabric.

⅛ yard *each* of 10 different retro prints for blocks*

½ yard of blue-and-orange floral for outer border

⅓ yard of cream fabric for blocks

¼ yard of medium blue fabric for inner border

⅓ yard of fabric for binding

1½ yards of fabric for backing

30" x 50" piece of batting

Or 1 strip, 2½" x 42", each of 10 different fabrics

Cutting

From the cream fabric, cut:
3 strips, 2½" x 42"; crosscut into 36 squares, 2½" x 2½"

From *each* of the 10 retro prints, cut:
1 strip, 2½" x 42"; crosscut into 4 rectangles, 2½" x 6½"
(40 total; 4 are extra)

From the medium blue fabric, cut:
3 strips, 1½" x 42"

From the blue-and-orange floral, cut:
4 strips, 3¾" x 42"

From the binding fabric, cut:
4 strips, 2¼" x 42"

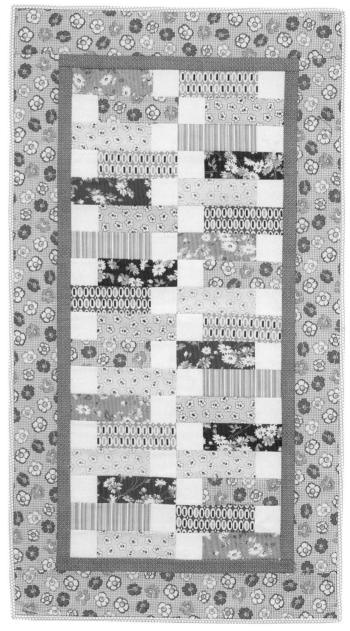

Pieced and quilted by Sara Diepersloot

Table-Runner Assembly

This is another project for which I love to use my design wall. (See "Making a Design Wall" on page 13.) Even though the fabrics in my table runner are laid out randomly, I still like to plan out the arrangement on my design wall. I want to make sure that the fabrics are scattered evenly throughout the runner, and that it is pleasing to the eye. So grab your fabrics and have fun with it!

1. Sew a cream square to one end of each of the 36 retro-print rectangles. Press the seam allowances toward the rectangles.

2. Join 18 units from step 1 into a row, paying special attention to the illustration and the orientation of the units. Make two rows. Press the rows in opposite directions. Sew the two rows together.

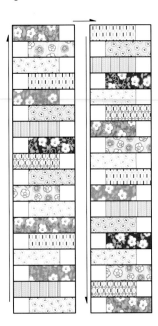

3. Referring to "Adding Borders" on page 13, attach the inner and outer borders.

4. Layer the quilt top with batting and backing, and quilt as desired.

5. Referring to "Binding" on page 14, bind the edges of the quilt.

Tilted Squares Table Runner

This table runner is quick to make and will aptly showcase a stunning fabric that you absolutely love!

Finished Table-Runner: 22½" x 54½"
Finished Block: 10" x 10"

Materials

Yardage is based on 42"-wide fabric.

⅝ yard of red poppy print for blocks and outer border

½ yard *OR* 1 fat quarter of black fabric for setting triangles

⅜ yard of red dot fabric for blocks

¼ yard of black dot fabric for blocks

¼ yard of black-and-gold print for inner border

¼ yard of red fabric for middle border

⅓ yard of fabric for binding

1¾ yards of fabric for backing

28" x 60" piece of batting

Cutting

From the red poppy print, cut:
1 strip, 6" x 42"; crosscut into 3 squares, 6" x 6"

4 strips, 3" x 42"

From the black dot fabric, cut:
1 strip, 4¾" x 42"; crosscut into 6 squares, 4¾" x 4¾".
Cut the squares once diagonally to make 12 triangles.

From the red dot fabric, cut:
3 strips, 3⅛" x 42"; crosscut into 12 rectangles, 3⅛" x 9⅜"

From the black fabric, cut:
1 square, 15½" x 15½"; cut twice diagonally to make 4 triangles

From the black-and-gold print, cut:
3 strips, 1½" x 42"

From the red fabric, cut:
3 strips, 1" x 42"

From the binding fabric, cut:
4 strips, 2¼" x 42"

Pieced and quilted by Sara Diepersloot

Making the Blocks

1. Sew a black dot triangle to each side of the red poppy squares. Press the seam allowances toward the black.

2. Cut the red dot rectangles in half diagonally as shown. You will use the triangles from the lower-right side. Put the other pieces aside for another project so that they don't get mixed up!

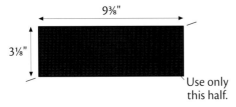

3. Sew a red triangle to each side of the blocks. They are a bit oversized to make sewing easier. Press the seam allowances toward the red.

4. Trim up the blocks to 10" x 10" square, making sure that you leave ¼" of red past the edges of the black square for your seam allowance.

Table-Runner Assembly

1. To assemble your table runner, sew the blocks and the black setting triangles into rows as shown. Join the rows. Refer to "Making Diagonally Set Quilts" on page 12 for additional help.

2. Sew a black-and-gold strip to the two long sides of the table runner, trimming the strip ends even with the runner edges. Press the seam allowances toward the border. Sew a black-and-gold strip to the right side of the point first, and trim even with the edges. Press the seam allowances toward the border. Add a black-and-gold strip to the left side; trim and press. Repeat for the other end of the table runner.

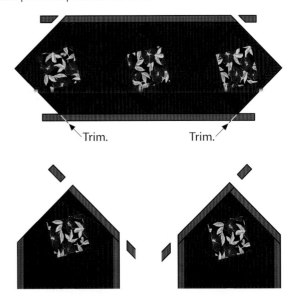

3. Repeat step 2 for the middle and outer borders.

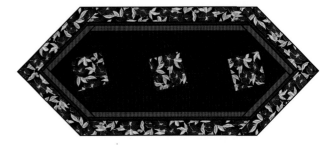

4. Layer the quilt top with batting and backing, and quilt as desired.

5. Referring to "Binding" on page 14, bind the edges of the quilt.

Cherries Table Runner

I love cherry print fabrics! This cute table runner will brighten up any room.

Finished Table Runner: 15½" x 38½"
Finished Block: 6" x 6"

Materials

Yardage is based on 42"-wide fabric.

½ yard of white-and-red dot fabric for blocks and setting triangles

⅓ yard of black-and-red cherry print for blocks and outer border

¼ yard of black dot fabric for block borders

¼ yard of red fabric for inner border

⅛ yard of red dot fabric for blocks

¼ yard of fabric for binding

1¼ yards of fabric for backing*

20" x 43" piece of batting

If you don't mind piecing the backing, ⅔ yard is enough, and depending on the width of your fabric, ⅝ yard may be enough.

Cutting

From the black-and-red cherry print, cut:
1 strip, 1½" x 42"
1 rectangle, 1½" x 3½"
3 strips, 2" x 42"

From the white-and-red dot fabric, cut:
1 strip, 1½" x 42"
1 rectangle, 1½" x 3½"
1 square, 12" x 12"; cut twice diagonally to make 4 triangles

From the red dot fabric, cut:
1 strip, 1½" x 42"
1 rectangle, 1½" x 3½"

From the black dot fabric, cut:
3 strips, 1¼" x 42"; crosscut into:
    6 rectangles, 1¼" x 6½"
    6 rectangles, 1¼" x 8"

From the red fabric, cut:
3 strips, 1¼" x 42"

From the binding fabric, cut:
3 strips, 2¼" x 42"

Making the Blocks

1. Join the 1½"-wide strips of cherry print, white-and-red dot fabric, and red dot fabric to make a strip set. Crosscut into 11 segments, 3½" wide. Make one additional segment using the 1½" x 3½" rectangles of the same fabrics.

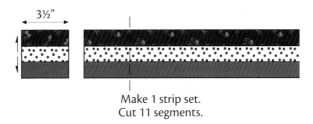

Make 1 strip set.
Cut 11 segments.

2. Join four segments from step 1 to make a block, rotating each segment as shown. Make three blocks.

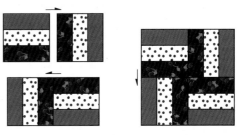

Make 3.

Pieced and quilted by Sara Diepersloot

3. Sew the 1¼" x 6½" black strips to opposite sides of the blocks. Press the seam allowances toward the black strip. Sew the 1¼" x 8" black strips to the top and bottom edges of each block. Press.

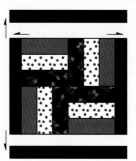

Table-Runner Assembly

1. To assemble your table runner, sew the blocks and setting triangles into rows as shown. Join the rows. Refer to "Making Diagonally Set Quilts" on page 12 for additional help.

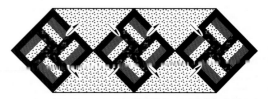

2. Sew a 1¼" red strip to each long side of the table runner, trimming the strip ends even with the runner edges. Press the seam allowances toward the border. Sew a 1¼" red strip to the right side of the point first, and trim even with the edges as shown on page 68 for the "Tilted Squares Table Runner." Press the seam allowances toward the border. Add a red print border strip to the left side; trim and press. Repeat for the other end of the table runner.

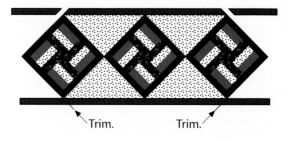

Trim.   Trim.

3. Repeat step 2 for the outer border.

4. Layer the quilt top with batting and backing, and quilt as desired.

5. Referring to "Binding" on page 14, bind the edges of the quilt.

Sweet Treats

I loved the colors in this whimsical cupcake fabric! This is an easy quilt that is set on the diagonal for added interest.

Finished Quilt: 66" x 66"
Finished Block: 12" x 12"

Materials

Yardage is based on 42"-wide fabric.

1¾ yards of cupcake print for blocks and border 4

1⅛ yards of red mottled print for blocks and setting triangles

⅞ yard of brown swirl print for blocks and border 3

⅝ yard of white-and-red dot fabric for blocks

⅜ yard of green print for blocks and border 2

⅓ yard of red-and-white striped fabric for border 1

¼ yard of red print for blocks

¼ yard of red checked fabric for blocks

⅛ yard of green checked fabric for blocks

⅝ yard of fabric for binding

4¼ yards of fabric for backing

72" x 72" piece of batting

Cutting

From the cupcake print, cut:
3 strips, 6½" x 42"; crosscut into 13 squares, 6½" x 6½"

7 strips, 5" x 42"

From the white-and-red dot fabric, cut:
9 strips, 2" x 42"; crosscut into 52 pieces, 2" x 6½"

From the red checked fabric, cut:
2 strips, 2" x 42"; crosscut into 36 squares, 2" x 2"

From the brown swirl print, cut:
9 strips, 2" x 42"; crosscut into 36 pieces, 2" x 9½"

6 strips, 1½" x 42"

From the red print, cut:
2 strips, 2" x 42"; crosscut into 36 squares, 2" x 2"

From the green checked fabric, cut:
1 strip, 2" x 42"; crosscut into 16 squares, 2" x 2"

From the red mottled print, cut:
4 strips, 2" x 42"; crosscut into 16 pieces, 2" x 9½"

2 squares, 18½" x 18½"; cut the squares twice diagonally to make 8 triangles

2 squares, 9½" x 9½"; cut the squares once diagonally to make 4 triangles

From the green print, cut:
1 strip, 2" x 42"; crosscut into 16 squares, 2" x 2"

6 strips, 1¼" x 42"

From the red-and-white striped fabric, cut:
6 strips, 1½" x 42"

From the binding fabric, cut:
7 strips, 2¼" x 42"

Making the Blocks

You will be making two blocks, A and B.

1. To make block A, sew white-and-red dot pieces to opposite sides of nine cupcake-print squares. Press the seam allowances toward the cupcake print.

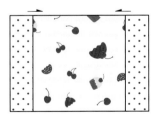

Pieced by Sara Diepersloot; quilted by Deborah Rasmussen

2. Sew a red checked square to each end of 18 white-and-red dot pieces. Press the seam allowances toward the red checked fabric. Join these units to the top and bottom edges of the blocks. Press the seam allowances toward the cupcake print.

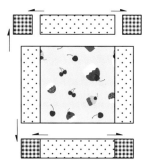

3. Join 2" x 9½" brown swirl pieces to opposite sides of the blocks. Press the seam allowances toward the brown swirl.

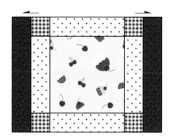

4. Sew a red print square to each end of the remaining 2" x 9½" brown swirl pieces. Press the seam allowances toward the brown swirl. Join these units to the top and bottom edges of the blocks. Press the seam allowances toward the brown swirl. Make nine of block A.

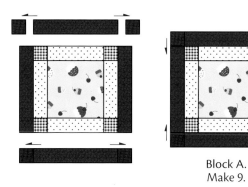

Block A.
Make 9.

5. To make block B, join white-and-red dot pieces to opposite sides of the four remaining cupcake-print squares. Press the seam allowances toward the cupcake print.

6. Sew a green checked square to each end of the remaining white-and-red dot pieces. Press the seam allowances toward the green checked fabric. Join these units to the top and bottom edges of the blocks. Press the seam allowances toward the cupcake print.

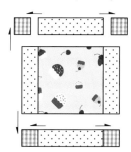

7. Join 2" x 9½" red mottled pieces to opposite sides of the blocks. Press the seam allowances toward the block center.

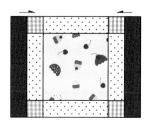

8. Sew a green print square to each end of the remaining 2" x 9½" red mottled pieces. Press the seam allowances toward the block center. Join these units to the top and bottom edges of the block. Press the seam allowances toward the block center. Make four of block B.

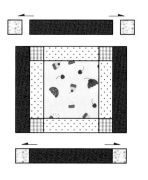
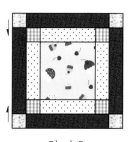

Block B.
Make 4.

Quilt-Top Assembly

1. Sew the blocks and setting triangles together into rows. Join the rows. Refer to "Making Diagonally Set Quilts" on page 12 for additional help.

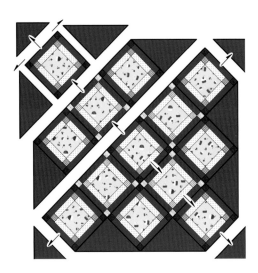

2. Referring to "Adding Borders" on page 13, attach the four rounds of borders.

3. Layer the quilt top with batting and backing, and quilt as desired.

4. Referring to "Binding" on page 14, bind the edges of the quilt.

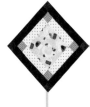

This red-and-green quilt could easily be made with Christmas fabrics for a fun holiday version. Or, use the red-and-white striped fabric as a jumping-off point for a picnic quilt.

I Love Recess!

I fell in love with this collection of fabric called "Recess," by Sandy Klop for Moda. This quilt uses one of those fabulous jelly rolls that have become so popular.

Finished Quilt: 66" x 66"
Finished Block: 18" x 18"

Materials

Yardage is based on 42"-wide fabric.

1 jelly roll with 36 fabrics OR 36 strips, 2½" x 42", for blocks

1⅛ yards of blue-and-orange floral for outer border

⅔ yard of muslin for blocks

⅜ yard of green print for inner border

⅝ yard of fabric for binding

4¼ yards of fabric for backing

72" x 72" piece of batting

Cutting

From *each* of the 2½" strips, cut:
1 piece, 2½" x 4½"

1 piece, 2½" x 6½"

1 piece, 2½" x 10½"

1 piece, 2½" x 14½"

From the muslin, cut:
8 strips, 2½" x 42"; crosscut into 117 squares, 2½" x 2½"

From the green print, cut:
6 strips, 1¾" x 42"

From the blue-and-orange floral, cut:
7 strips, 5" x 42"

From the binding fabric, cut:
7 strips, 2¼" x 42"

Making the Blocks

I used my design wall to decide the fabric placement within each block. (See "Making a Design Wall" on page 00.) This is a scrappy quilt, but I wanted to make sure that the fabrics were distributed evenly throughout. The blocks are assembled from the center outward, counterclockwise in rounds using a partial seam. When adding the rounds, press all seam allowances away from the center.

1. Layer a muslin square and a 2½" x 4½" piece right sides together as shown. Sew until you are approximately 1" from the bottom edge of the muslin square. Leave the rest of the seam unsewn. You will finish the seam when you sew the last piece of each round. Finger-press the seam allowance away from the muslin.

2. Join a 2½" x 4½" piece to the top edge of the unit from step 1. Press.

3. Join a 2½" x 4½" piece to the left side of the unit. Press.

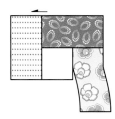

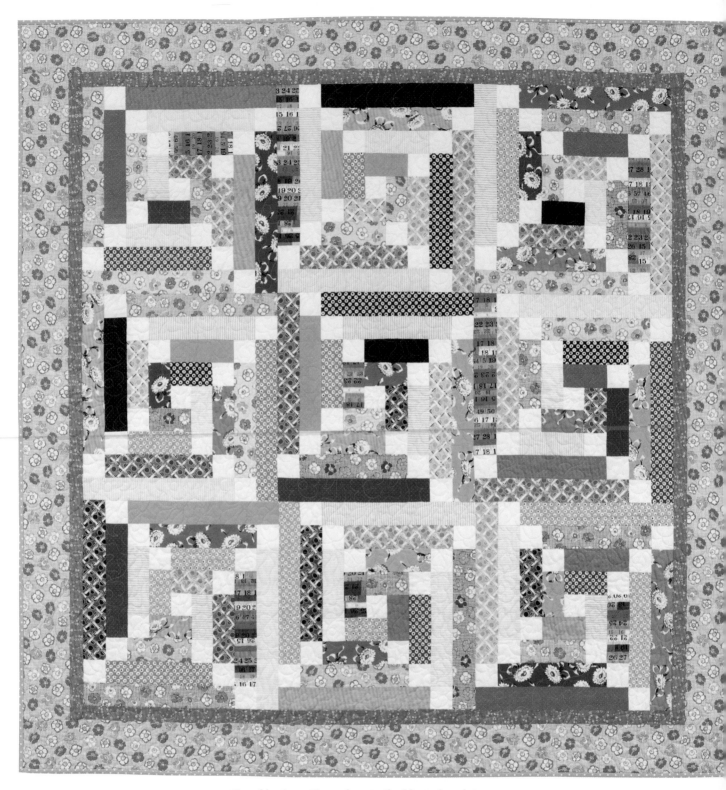

Pieced by Sara Diepersloot; quilted by Deborah Rasmussen

4. Join a 2½" x 4½" piece to the bottom edge of the unit, folding the first rectangle back out of the way. Press.

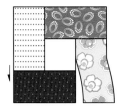

5. Sew the remainder of the seam that was left unsewn in step 1. Press.

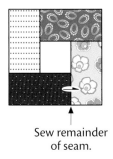

Sew remainder
of seam.

6. Sew muslin squares to one end of *all* the 2½" x 6½", 2½" x 10½", and 2½" x 14½" pieces. Press the seam allowances away from the muslin.

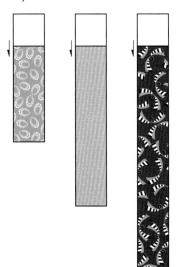

7. Add the next round, using the 2½" x 6½" pieces with muslin squares from step 6. Repeat steps 1–5, leaving the first seam partially unsewn as you did before.

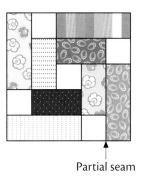

Partial seam

8. Add the next round in the same manner, using the 2½" x 10½" pieces with muslin squares from step 6. Remember to leave the first seam partially unsewn.

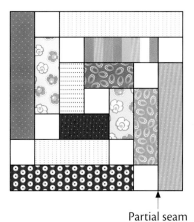

Partial seam

9. Add the last round, using the 2½" x 14½" pieces with muslin squares from step 6; remember to leave the first seam partially unsewn. Make a total of nine blocks.

Make 9.

Partial seam

Quilt-Top Assembly

1. Join three blocks to make a row. Make three rows. Press the seam allowances in the opposite direction from row to row. Sew the rows together.

2. Referring to "Adding Borders" on page 13, attach the inner and outer borders.

3. Layer the quilt top with batting and backing, and quilt as desired.

4. Referring to "Binding" on page 14, bind the edges of the quilt.

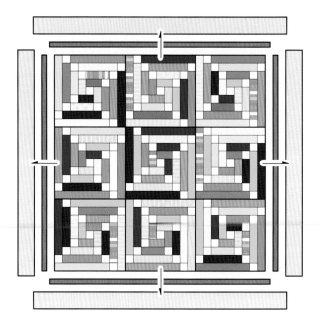

Sometimes picking out all of the fabrics for a quilt can be daunting. Using a jelly roll takes out all of the guesswork for you! It is a fun, fast way to incorporate a lot of different fabrics into your project that all coordinate beautifully.

About the Author

SARA DIEPERSLOOT lives in Scotts Valley, California, with her husband, Rodney, and four beautiful children: Laura, Kimmie, Ryan, and David. She has had a passion for sewing and design since she was a young girl. This passion led her to get her degree in fashion design and pattern making from the Fashion Institute of Design and Merchandising in San Francisco. She worked in the fashion industry for several years before starting her family. Her love of sewing brought her to the local quilt shop to learn how to quilt, and after making her first baby quilt, she was hooked!

Sara loves to scour the quilt shops for new fabrics and inspiration, and she especially enjoys incorporating novelty and large-scale prints into her designs. Being a busy mom, she knows the importance of designing quilts that are easy to complete but still satisfy the desire to make something beautiful.

Sara is a full-time mom, chauffeur, cook, homework helper, and now author. She loves to hang out with her family, ride bikes with her kids, cook, read, knit, travel, and, of course, quilt!

Photo by Erica Sergio

New and Best-Selling Titles from

That Patchwork Place®

America's Best-Loved
Quilt Books®

Martingale®
& COMPANY

America's Best-Loved Craft & Hobby Books®
America's Best-Loved Knitting Books®

APPLIQUÉ
Appliqué Quilt Revival
Beautiful Blooms
Cutting-Garden Quilts
Dream Landscapes
Easy Appliqué Blocks
Simple Comforts
Sunbonnet Sue and Scottie Too

BABIES AND CHILDREN
Baby's First Quilts
Let's Pretend
Snuggle-and-Learn Quilts for Kids
Sweet and Simple Baby Quilts
Warm Welcome—NEW!

BEGINNER
Color for the Terrified Quilter
Four-Patch Frolic—NEW!
Happy Endings, Revised Edition
Machine Appliqué for the Terrified Quilter
Quilting Your Style—NEW!
Your First Quilt Book (or it should be!)

GENERAL QUILTMAKING
American Jane's Quilts for All Seasons
Bits and Pieces
Bold and Beautiful
Country-Fresh Quilts
Creating Your Perfect Quilting Space
Fat-Quarter Quilting—NEW!
Fig Tree Quilts: Fresh Vintage Sewing
Folk-Art Favorites
Follow-the-Line Quilting Designs
    Volume Three
Gathered from the Garden
The New Handmade
Points of View
Prairie Children and Their Quilts
Quilt Challenge—NEW!
Quilt Revival
A Quilter's Diary
Quilter's Happy Hour

Quilting for Joy
Quilts from Paradise—NEW!
Remembering Adelia
Simple Seasons
Skinny Quilts and Table Runners
Twice Quilted

HOLIDAY AND SEASONAL
Candy Cane Lane—NEW!
Christmas Quilts from Hopscotch
Comfort and Joy
Deck the Halls—NEW!
Holiday Wrappings

HOOKED RUGS, NEEDLE FELTING, AND PUNCHNEEDLE
Miniature Punchneedle Embroidery
Needle Felting with Cotton and Wool
Needle-Felting Magic

PAPER PIECING
A Year of Paper Piecing
Easy Reversible Vests, Revised Edition
Paper-Pieced Mini Quilts
Show Me How to Paper Piece

PIECING
501 Rotary-Cut Quilt Blocks
Favorite Traditional Quilts Made Easy
Loose Change
Mosaic Picture Quilts
New Cuts for New Quilts
On-Point Quilts
Ribbon Star Quilts
Rolling Along

QUICK QUILTS
40 Fabulous Quick-Cut Quilts
Charmed, I'm Sure—NEW!
Instant Bargello
Quilts on the Double
Sew Fun, Sew Colorful Quilts
Supersize 'Em!

SCRAP QUILTS
Nickel Quilts
Save the Scraps
Scrap-Basket Surprises
Simple Strategies for Scrap Quilts

CRAFTS
A to Z of Sewing
Art from the Heart
The Beader's Handbook
Dolly Mama Beads
Embellished Memories
Friendship Bracelets All Grown Up
Making Beautiful Jewelry
Paper It!
Trading Card Treasures

KNITTING & CROCHET
365 Crochet Stitches a Year
365 Knitting Stitches a Year
A to Z of Knitting
All about Crochet—NEW!
All about Knitting
Amigurumi World
Amigurumi Two!—NEW!
Beyond Wool
Cable Confidence
Casual, Elegant Knits
Crocheted Pursenalities
Knitted Finger Puppets
The Knitter's Book of Finishing
    Techniques
Knitting Circles around Socks
*Knitting More Circles around
    Socks—NEW!*
Knits from the North Sea—NEW!
More Sensational Knitted Socks
*New Twists on Twined Knitting—
    NEW!*
Pursenalities
Simple Stitches
Toe-Up Techniques for Hand-
    Knit Socks, Revised Edition
Together or Separate

Our books are available at bookstores and your favorite craft, fabric, and yarn retailers. If you don't see the title you're looking for, visit us at **www.martingale-pub.com** or contact us at:

1-800-426-3126

International: 1-425-483-3313
Fax: 1-425-486-7596 • Email: info@martingale-pub.com